ANIMAL
ABC COLORING BOOK
AND
123 NUMBERS

T. Michelle

Published by PUBLISHING COMPANY in 2016
First edition: First printing
Illustrations and design © 2016 T.Michelle

Author Contact
Best Book By T. Michelle
(fb.com/groups/1523056898003358)

ISBN-13: 978-1533007278
ISBN-10: 1533007276

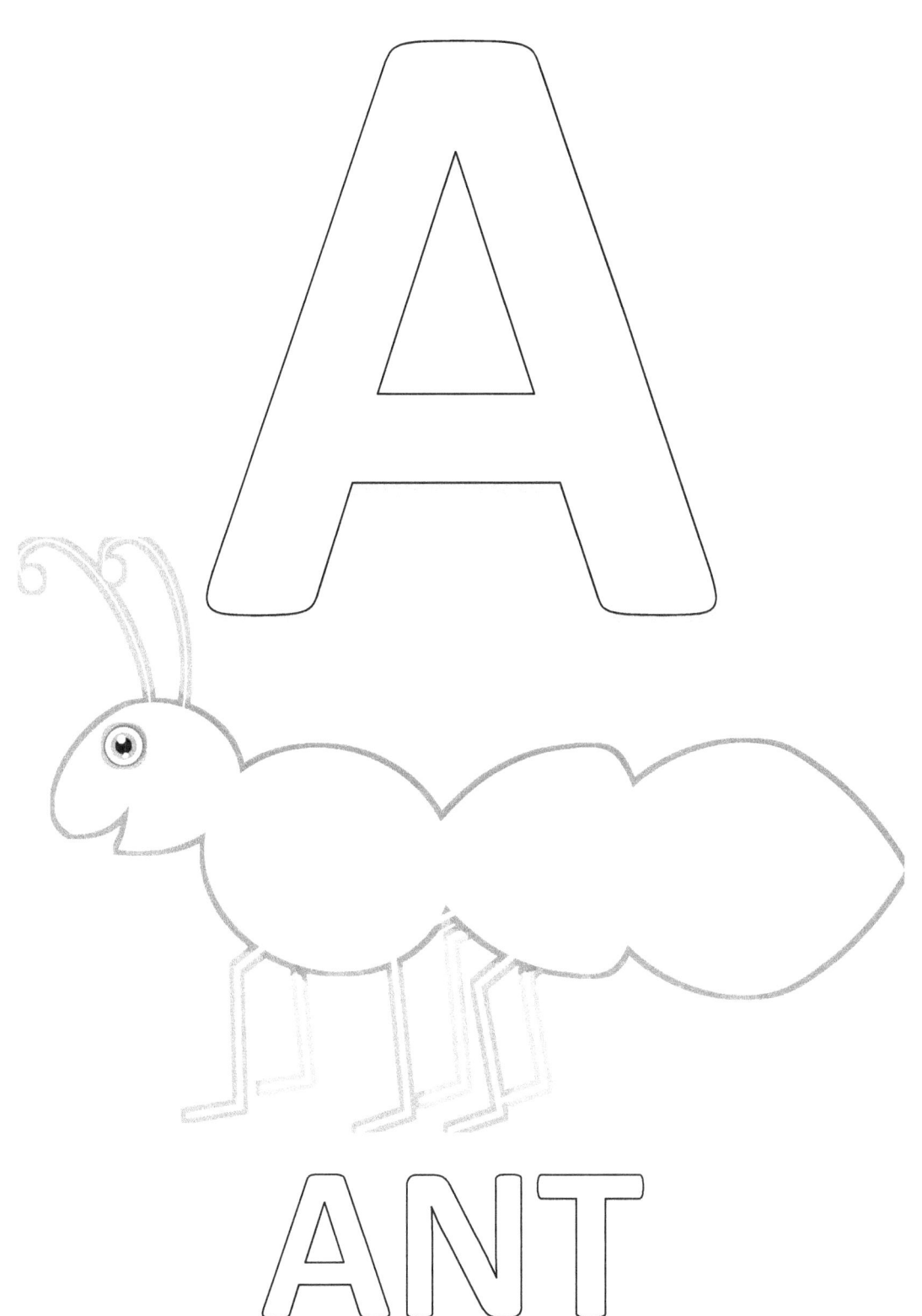

ANT

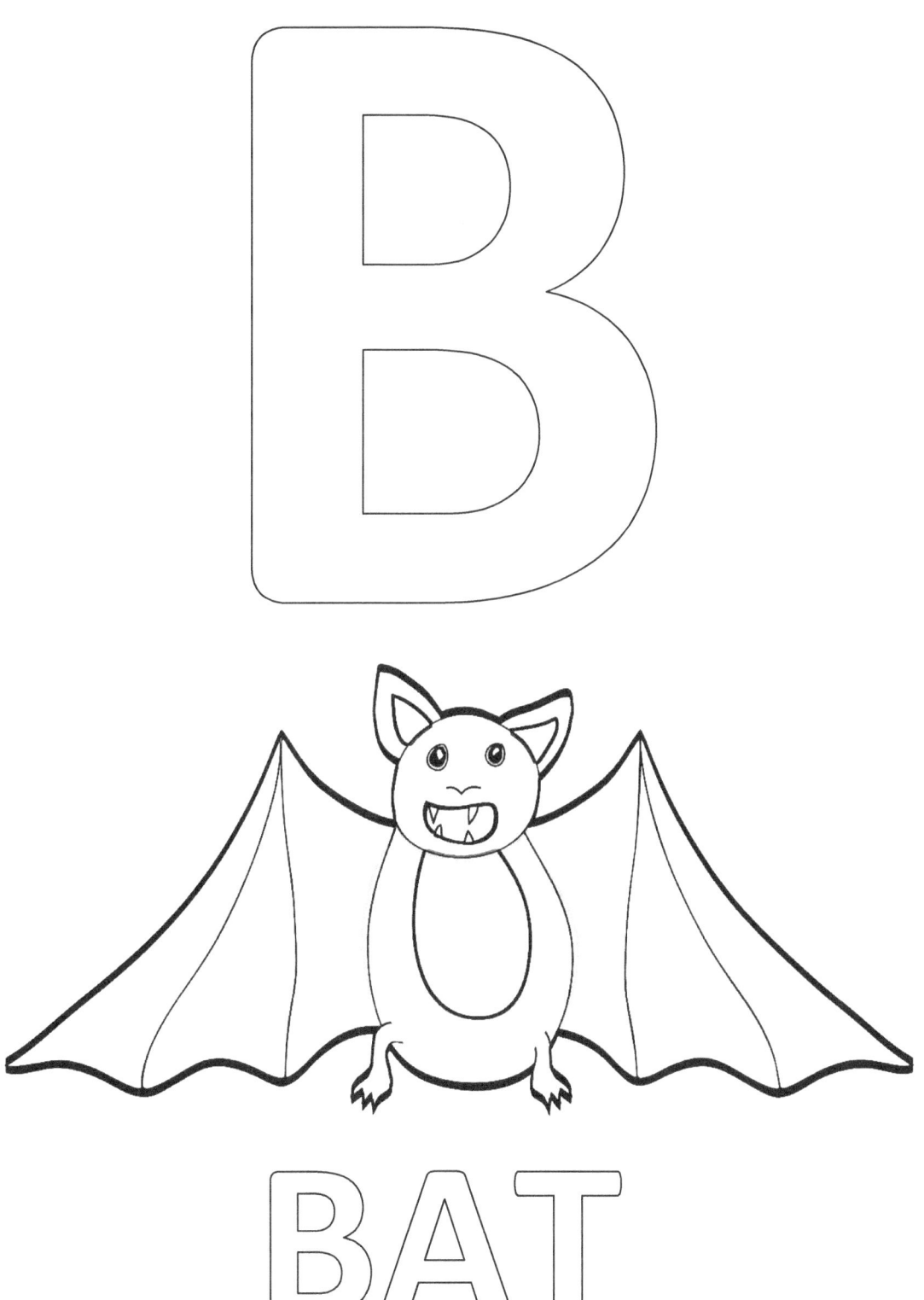

B

BAT

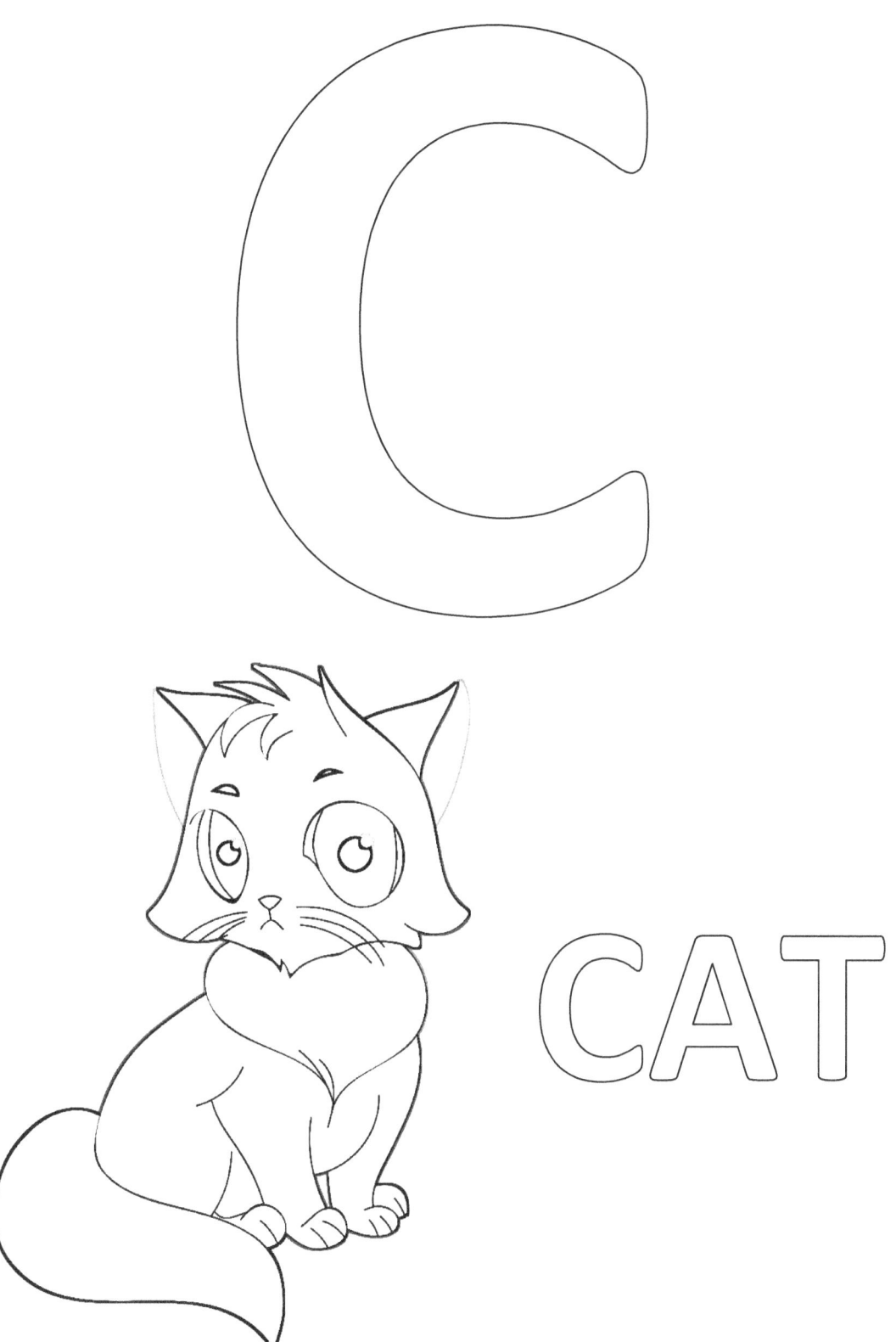

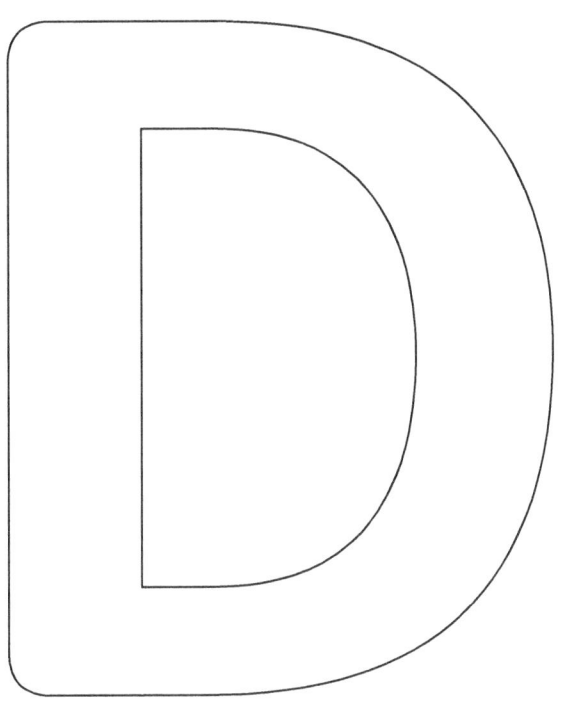

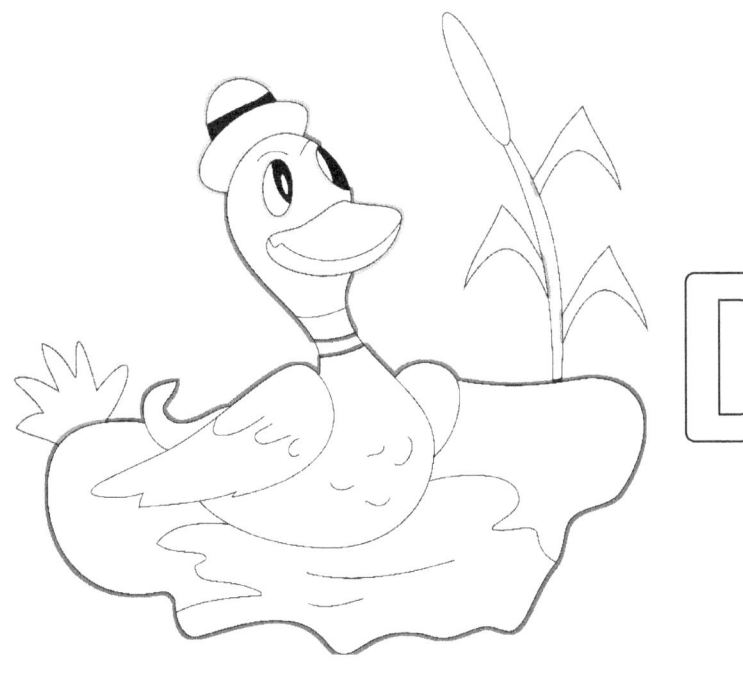

DUCK

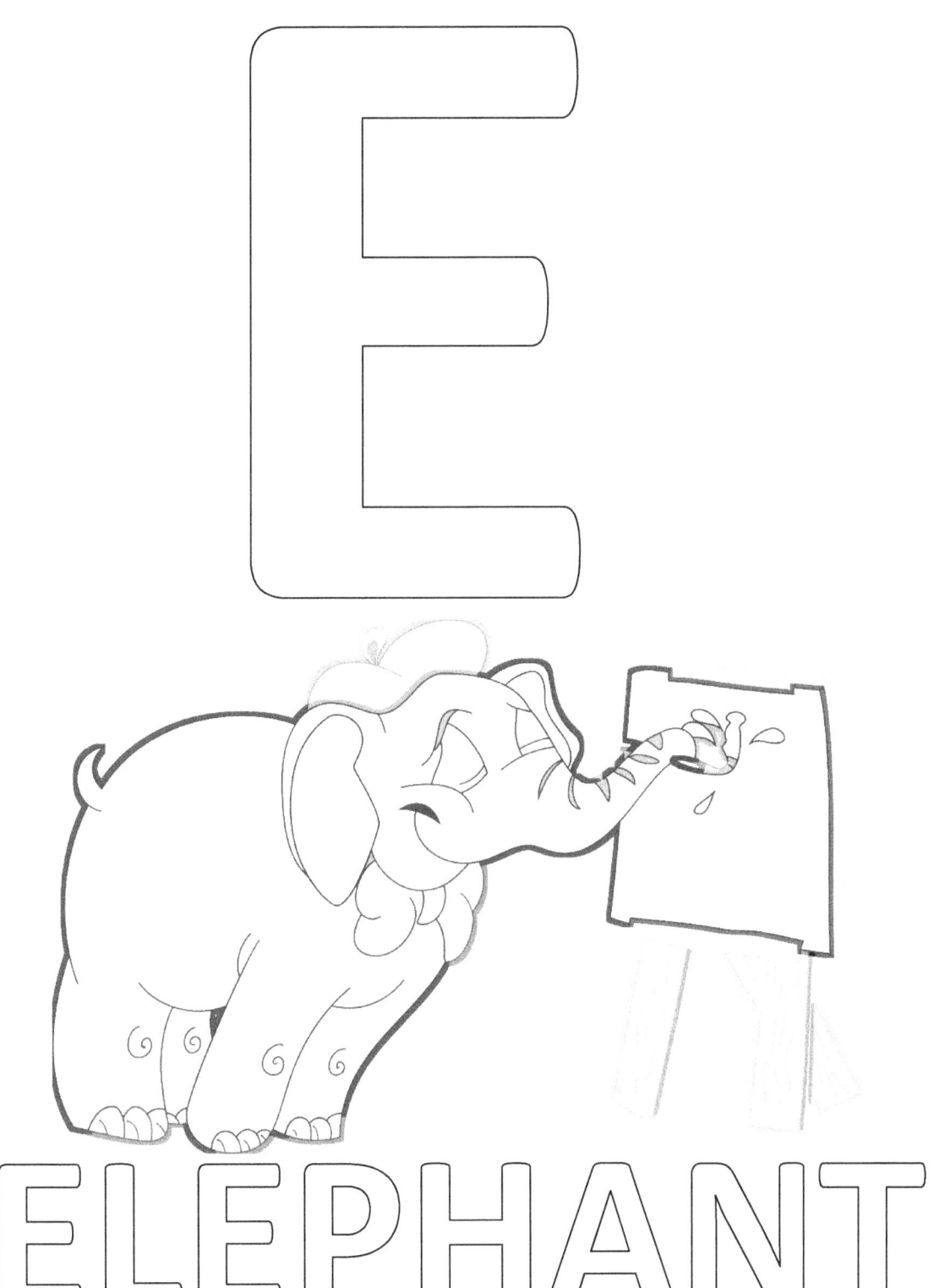

E

ELEPHANT

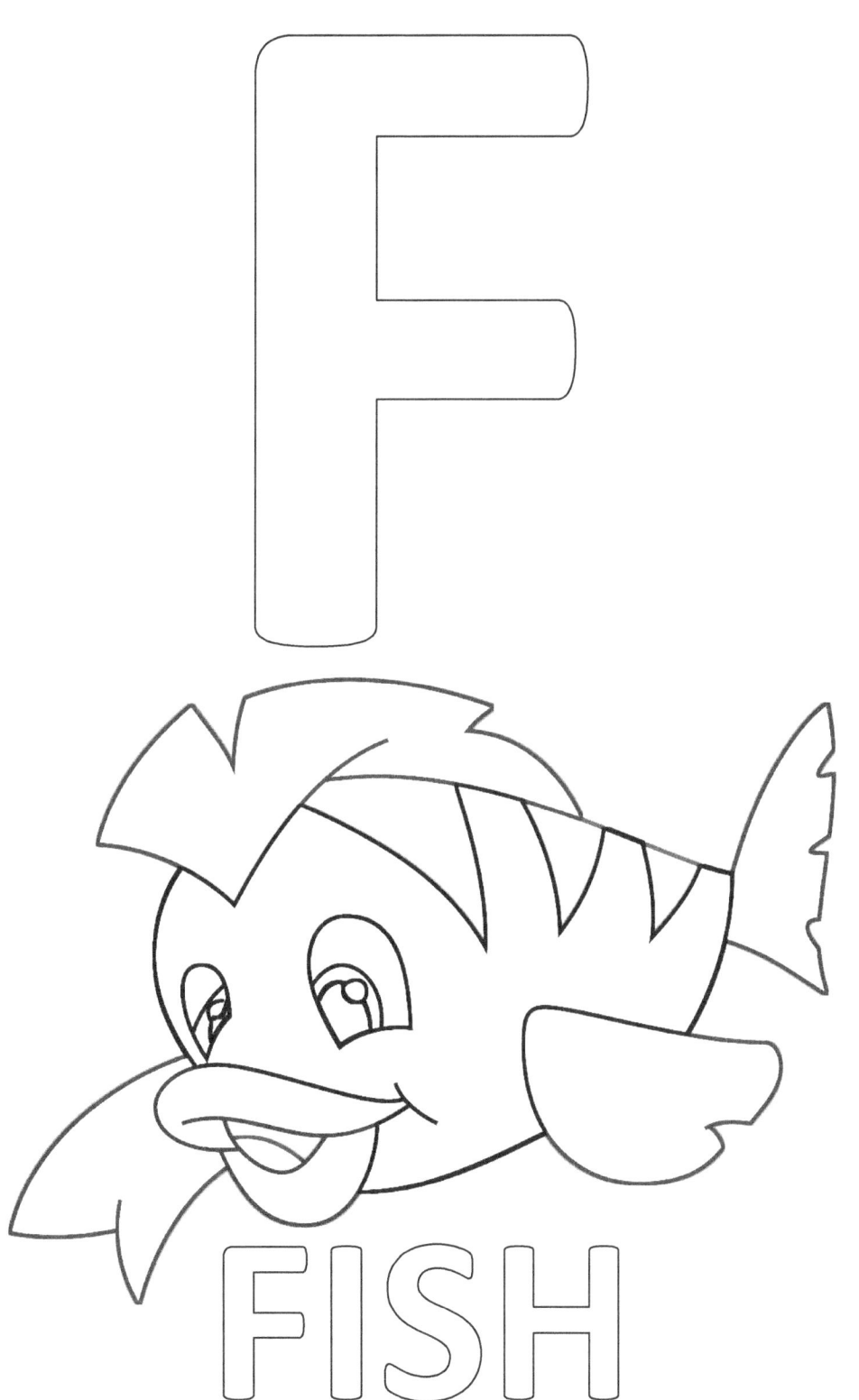

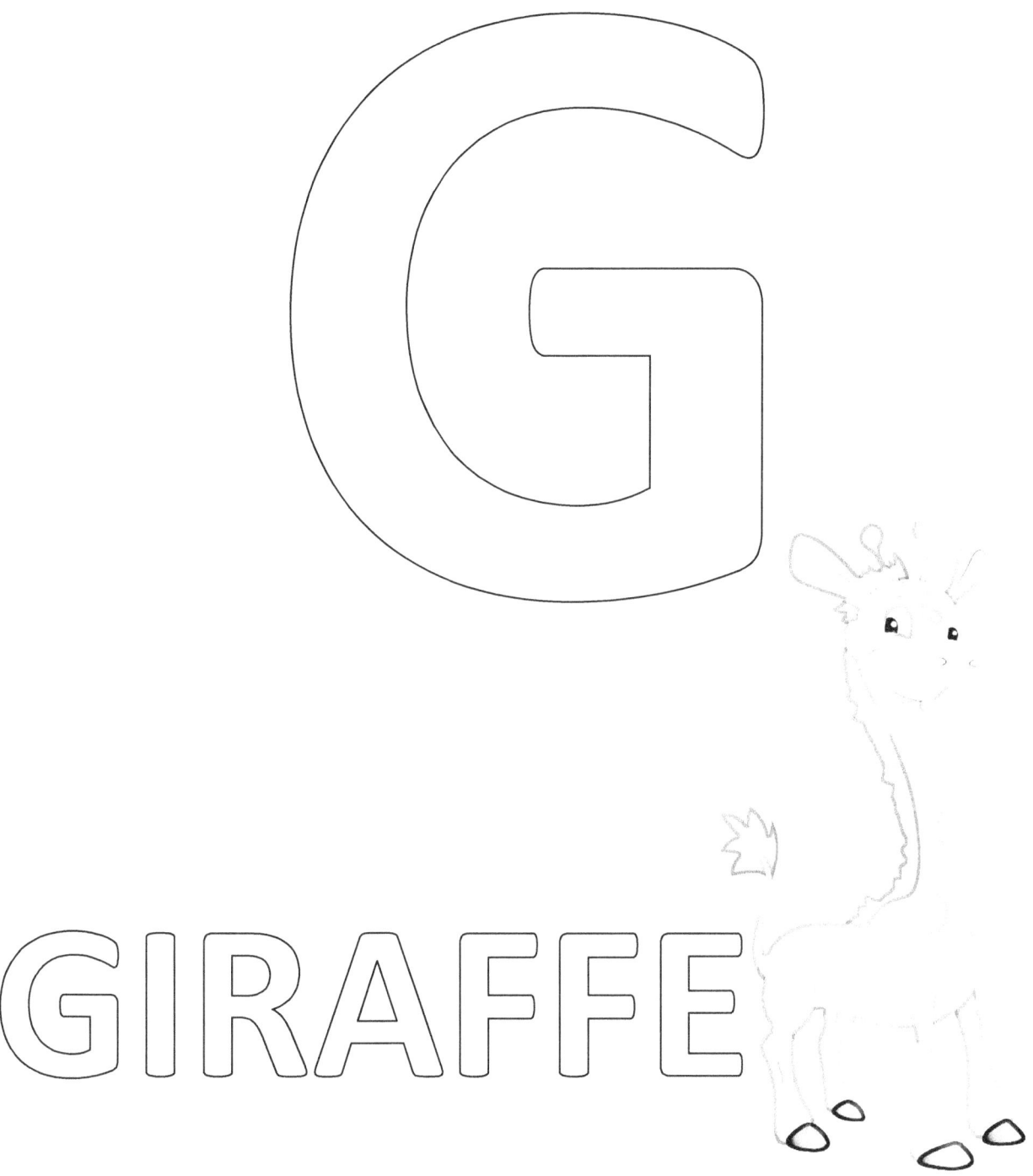

GIRAFFE

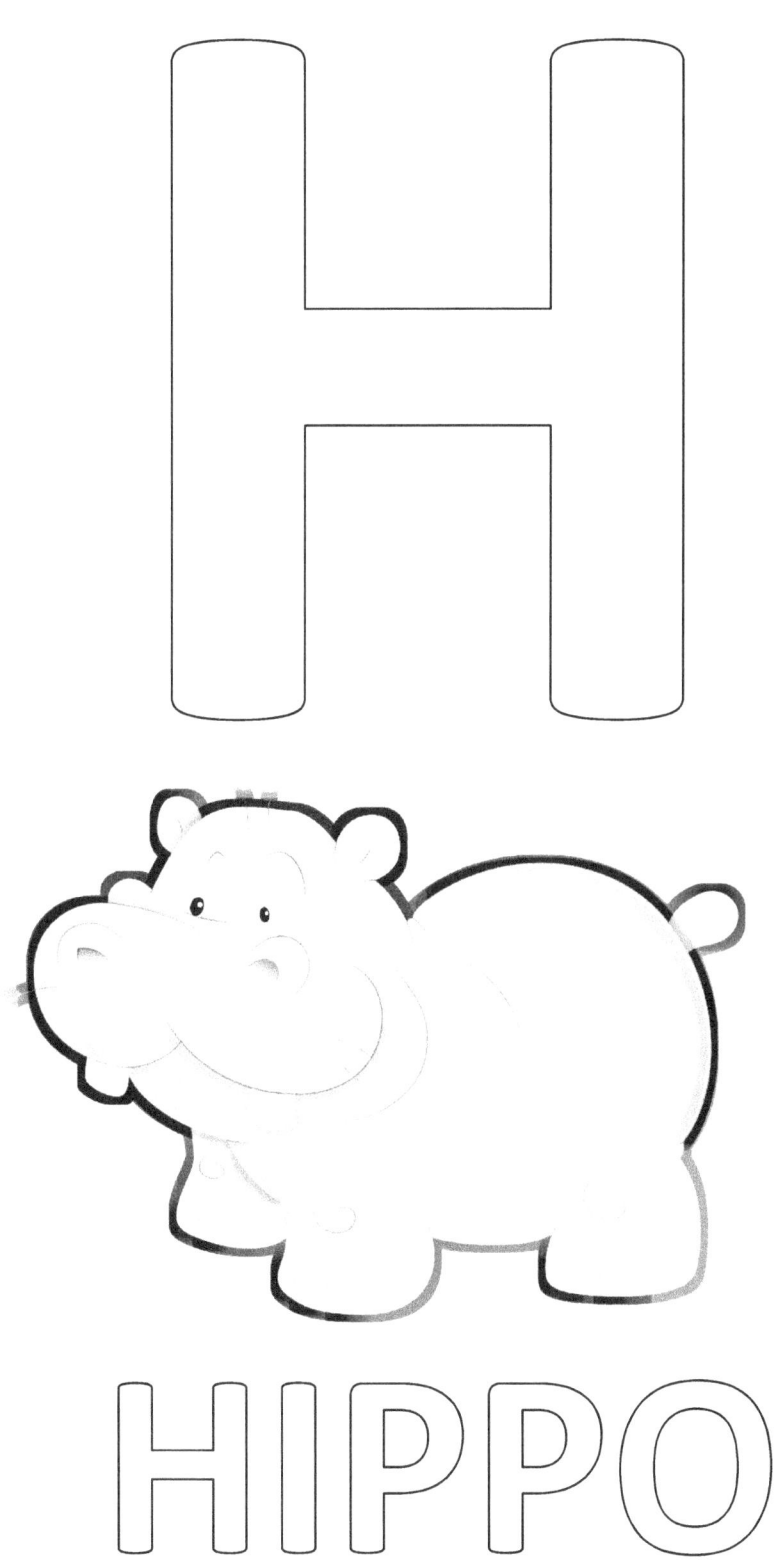

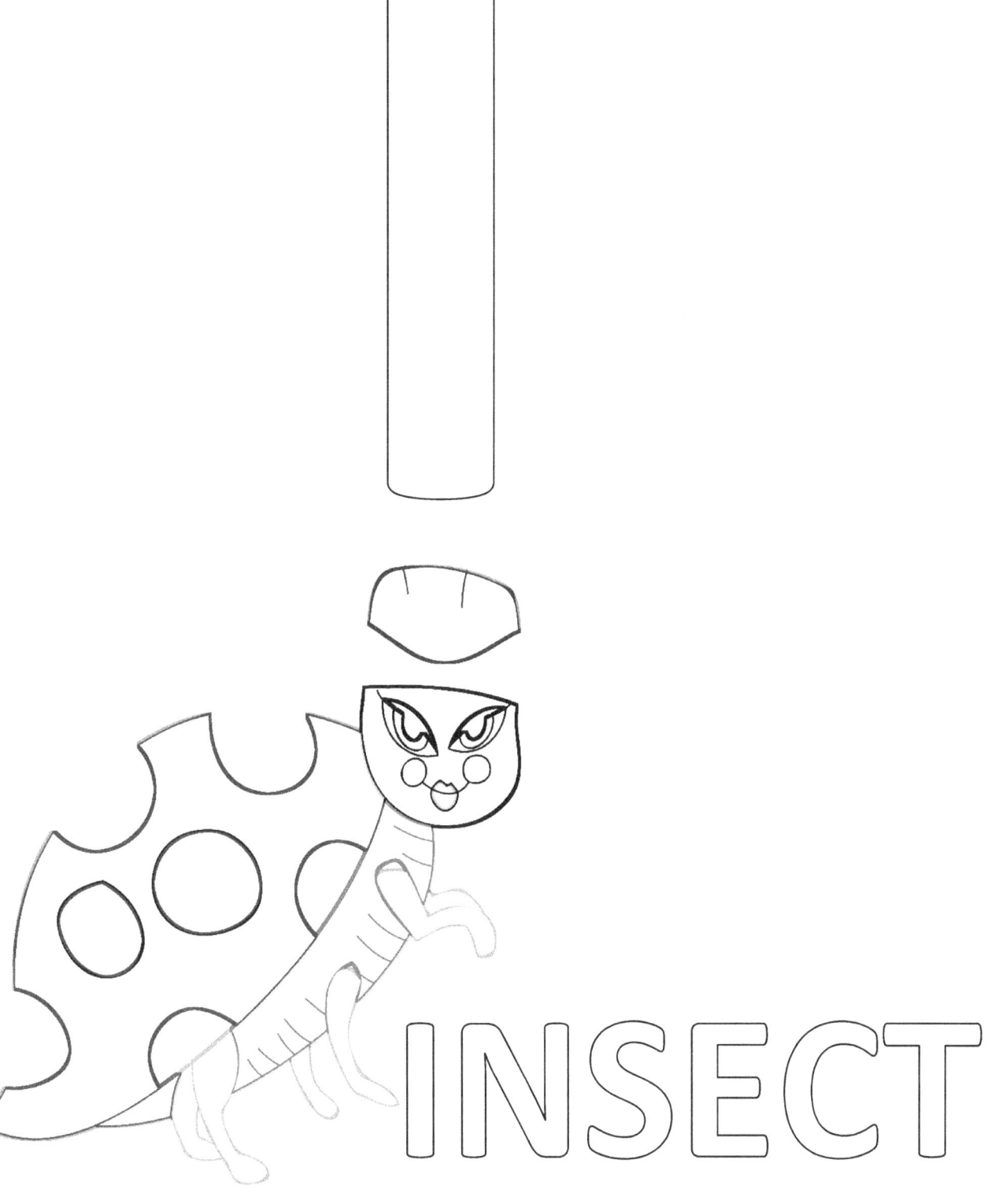

INSECT

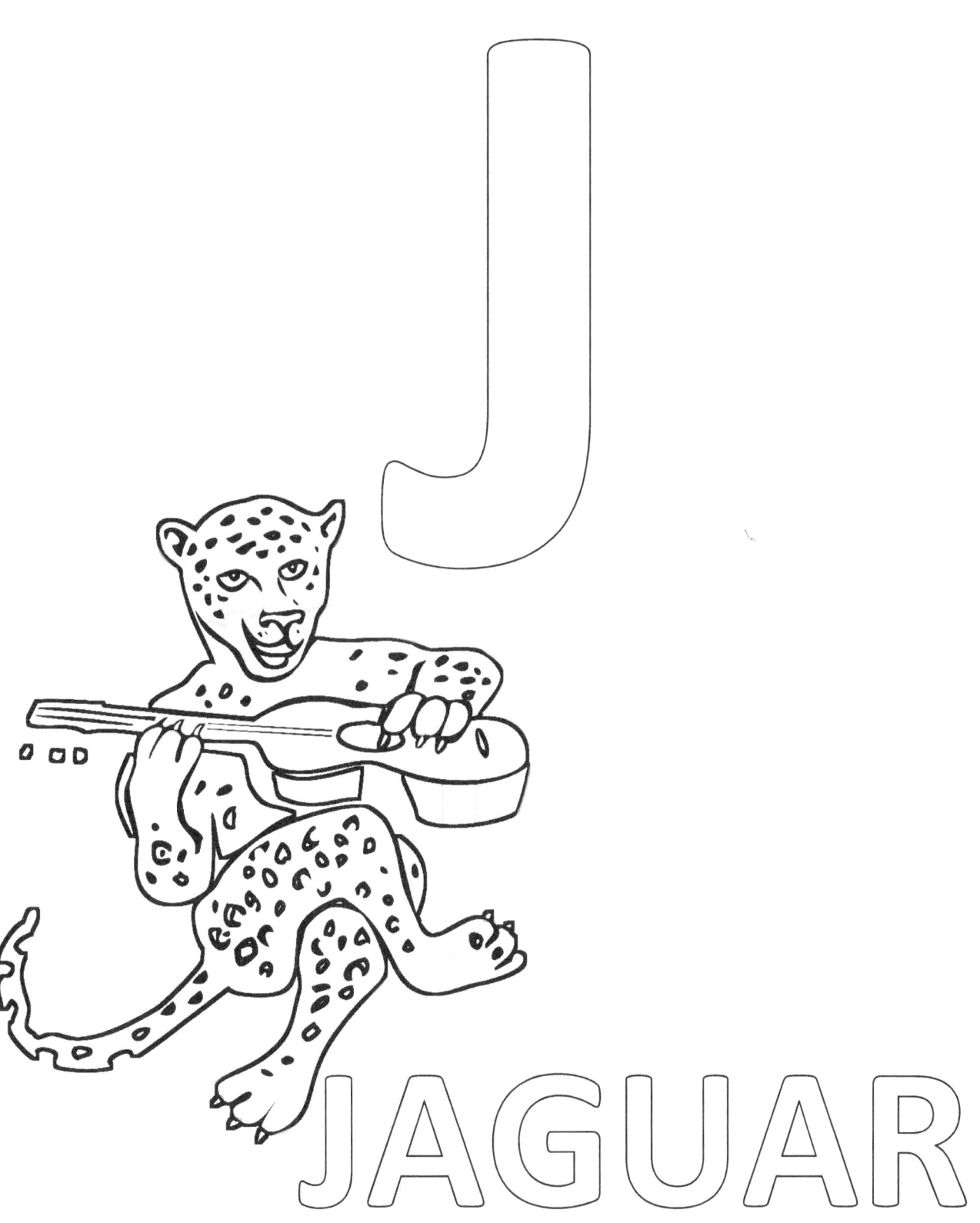

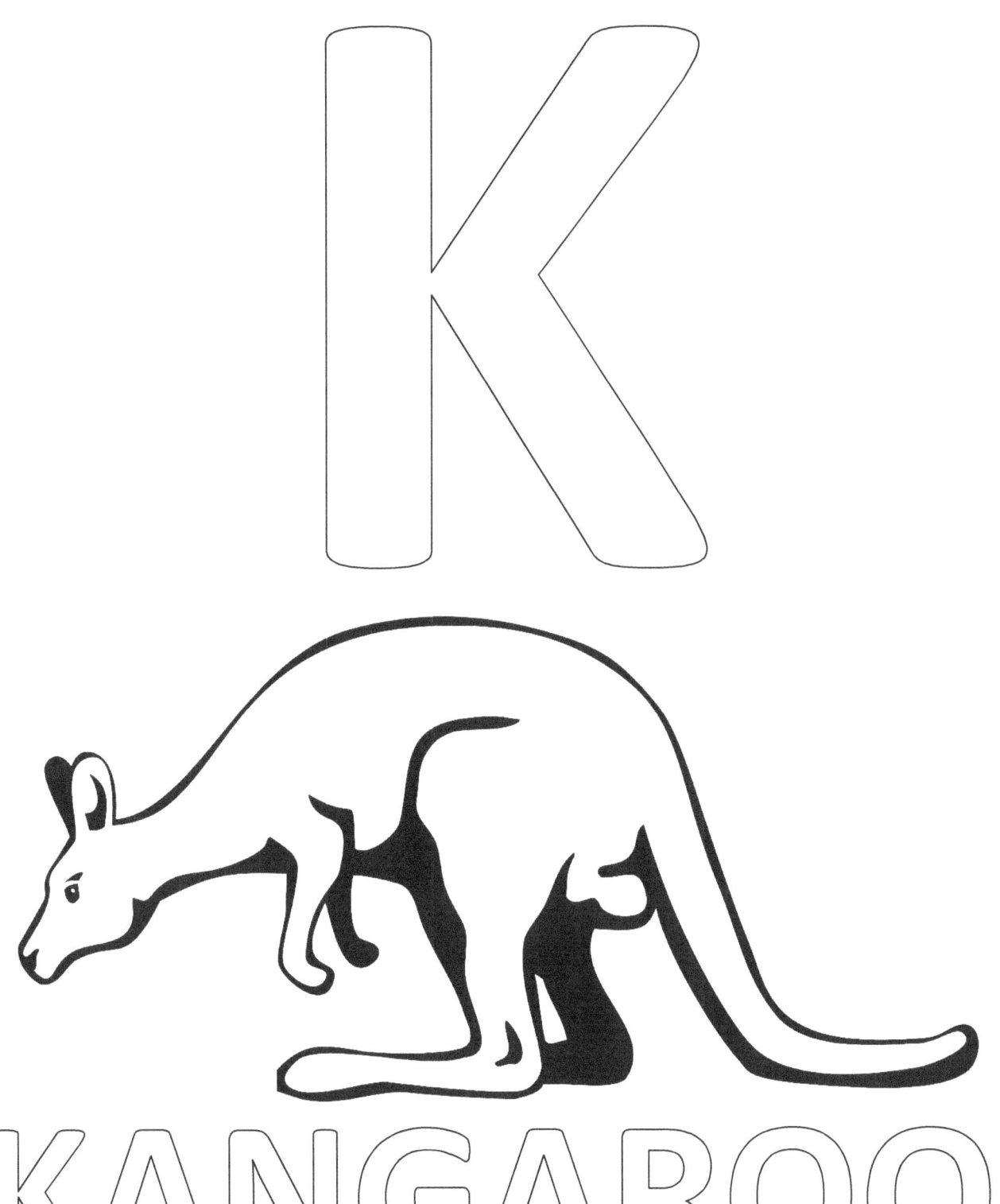

K

KANGAROO

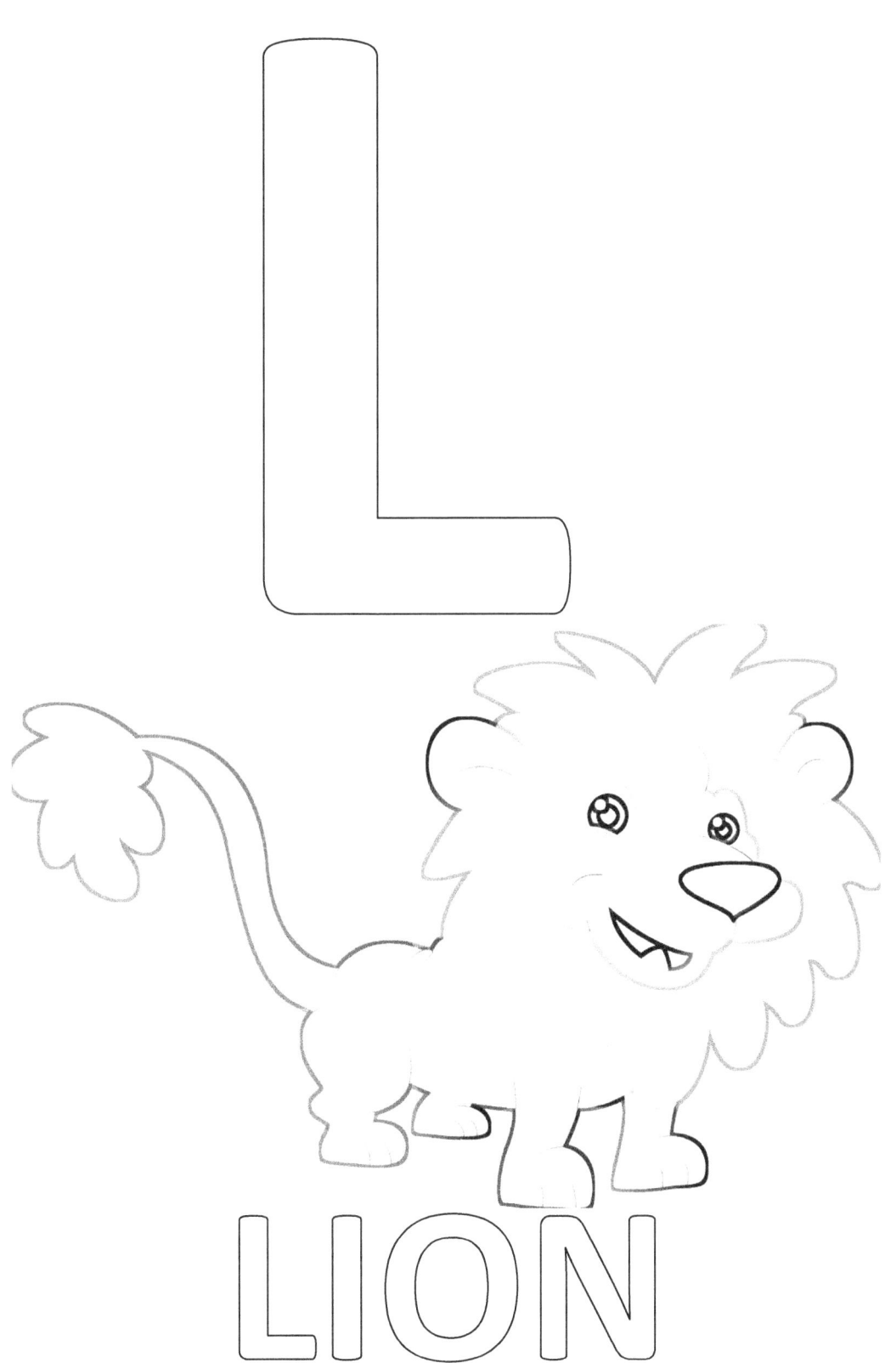

LION

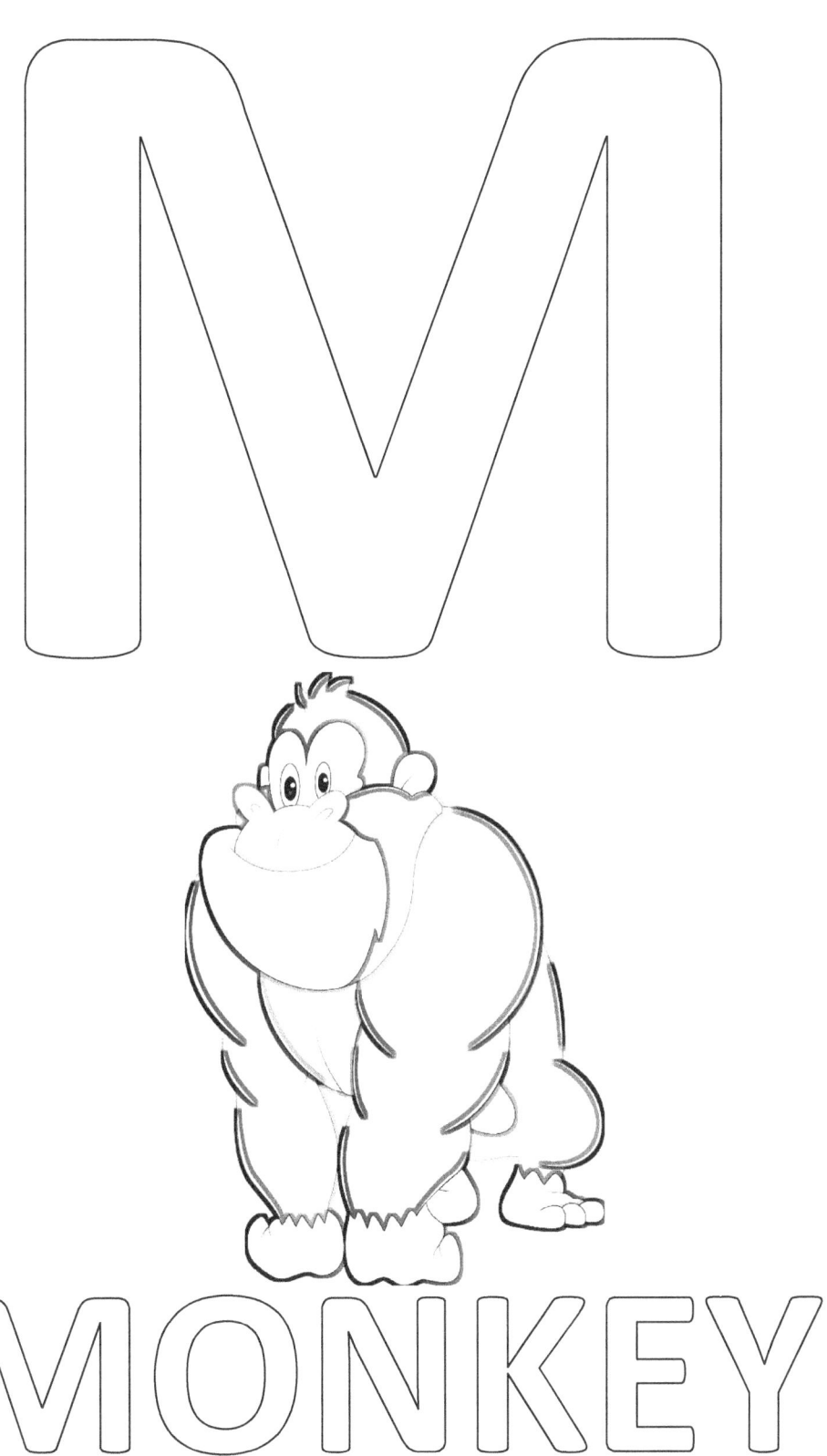

MONKEY

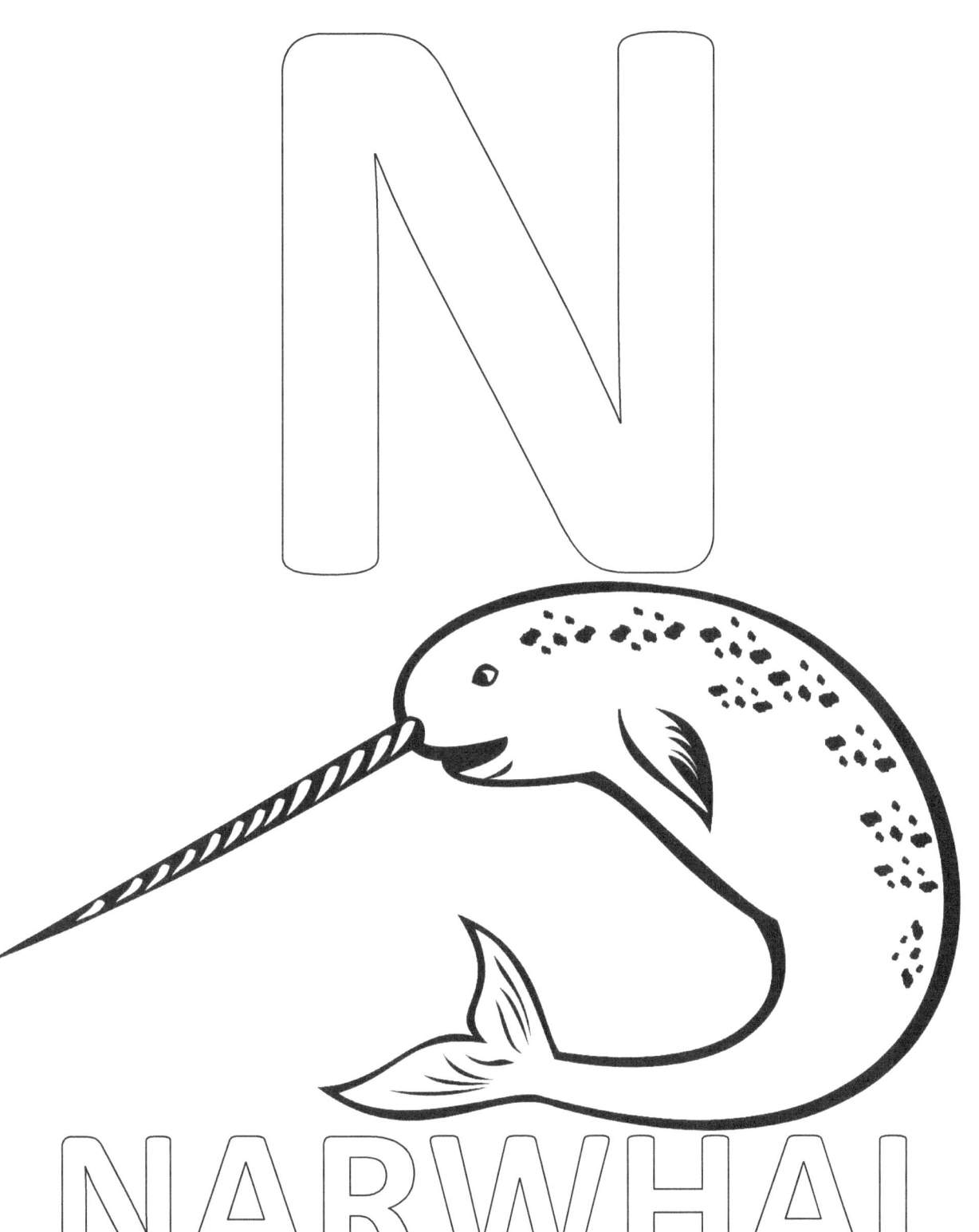

NARWHAL

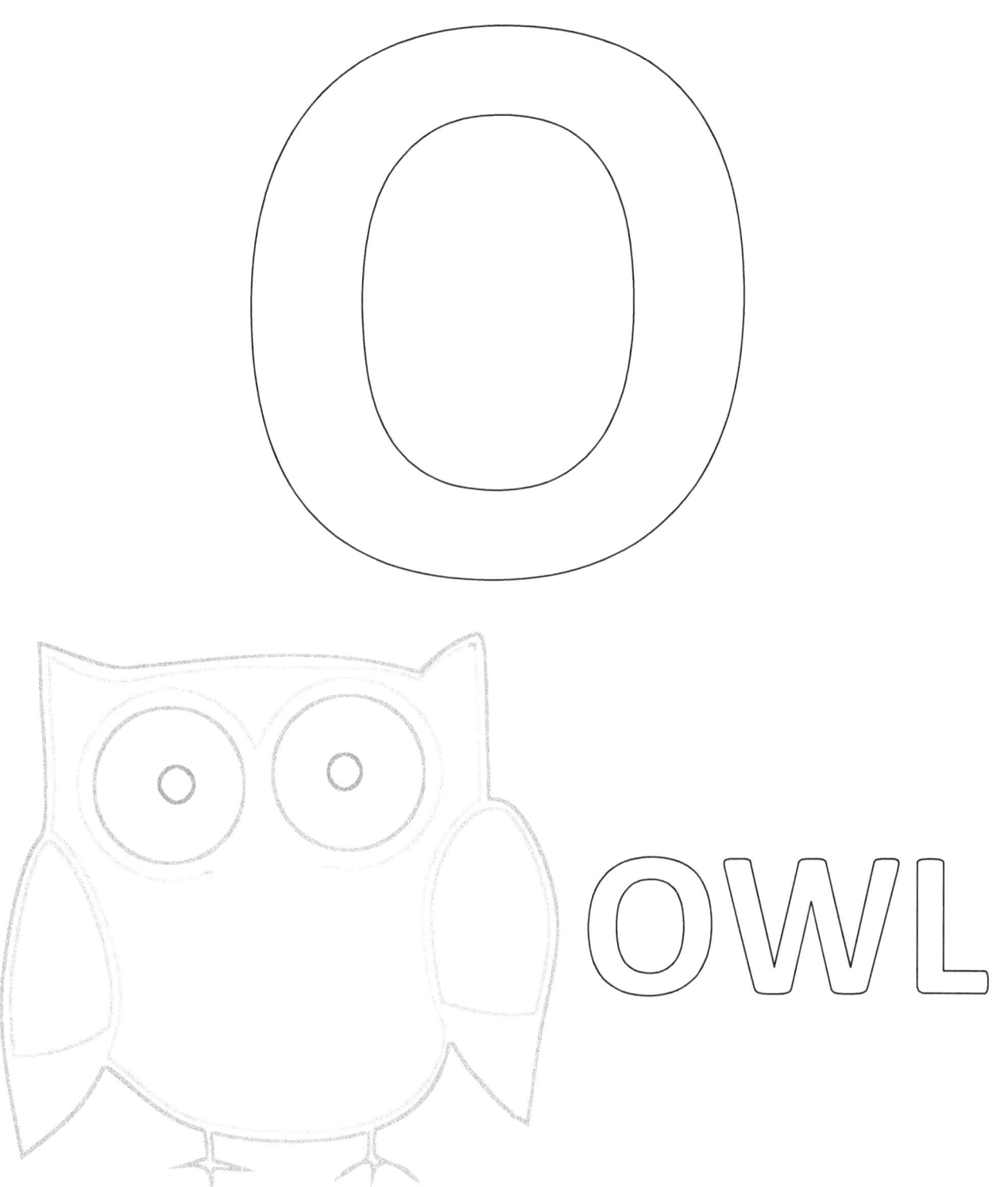

O

OWL

P

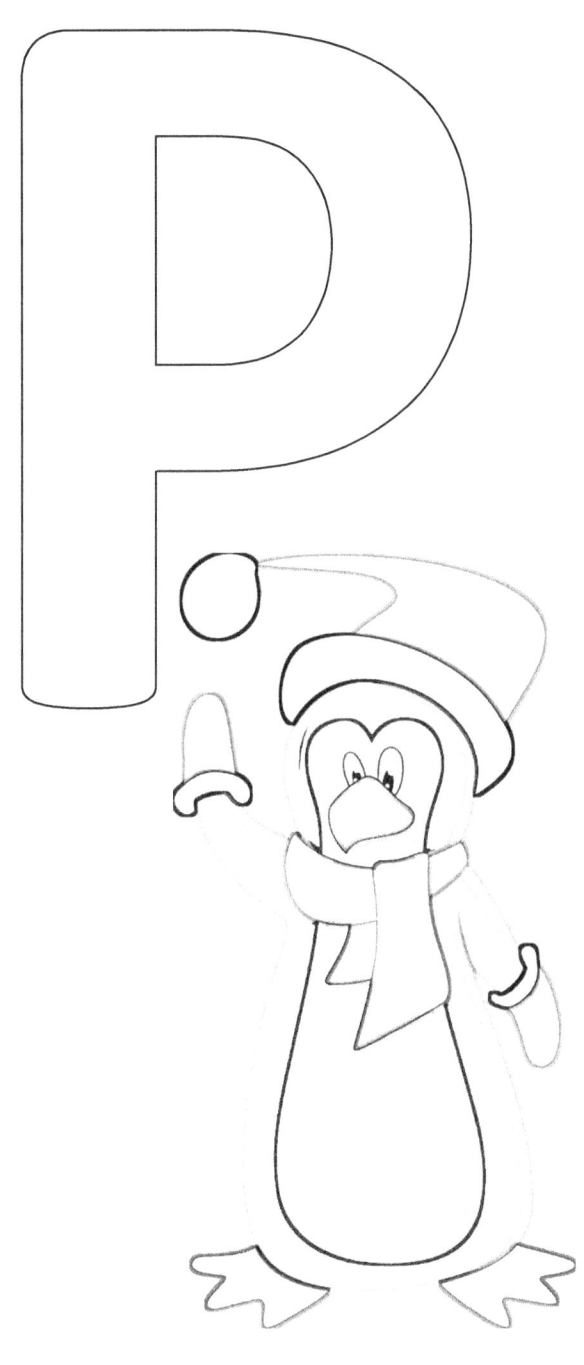

PENGUIN

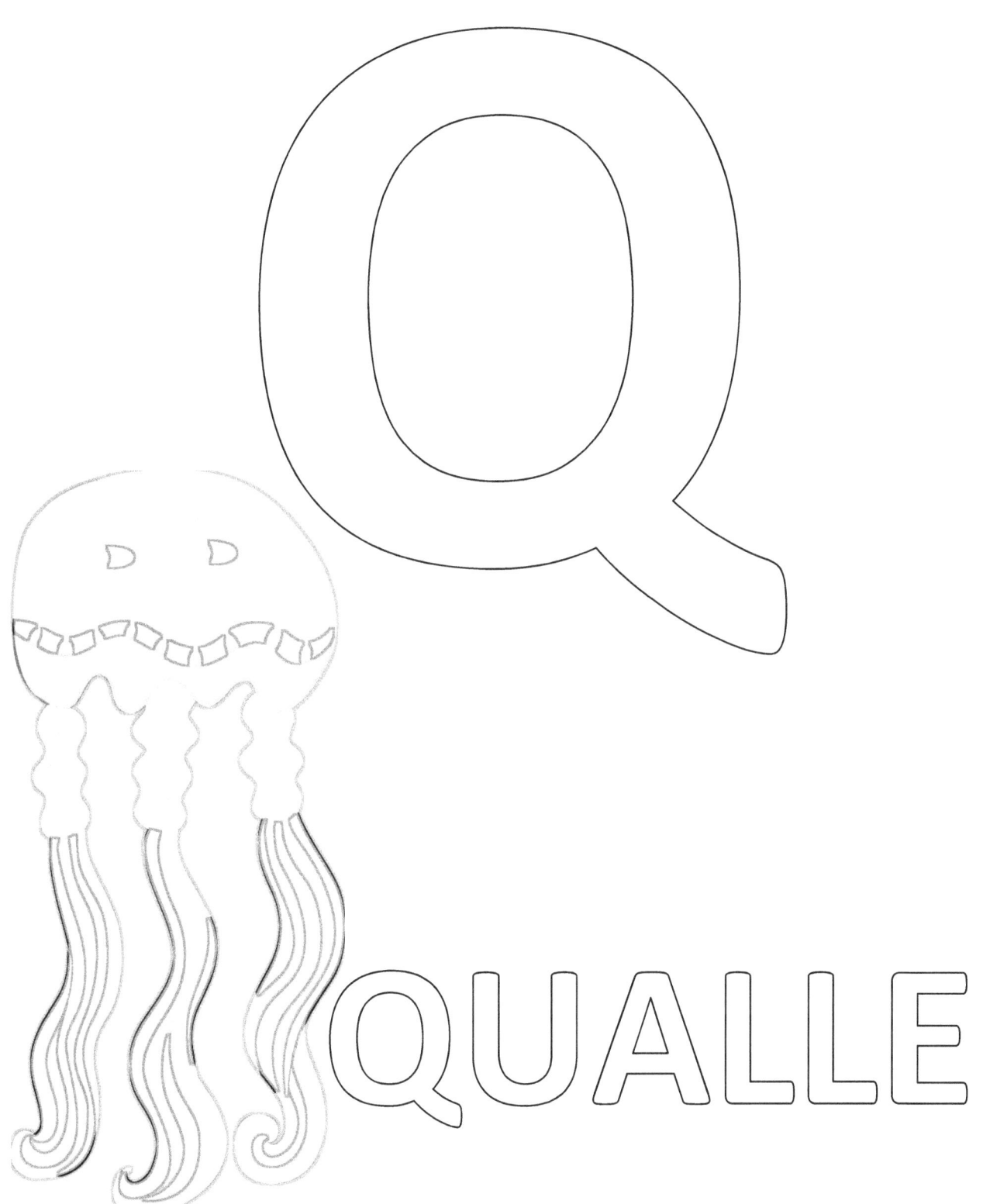

Q

QUALLE

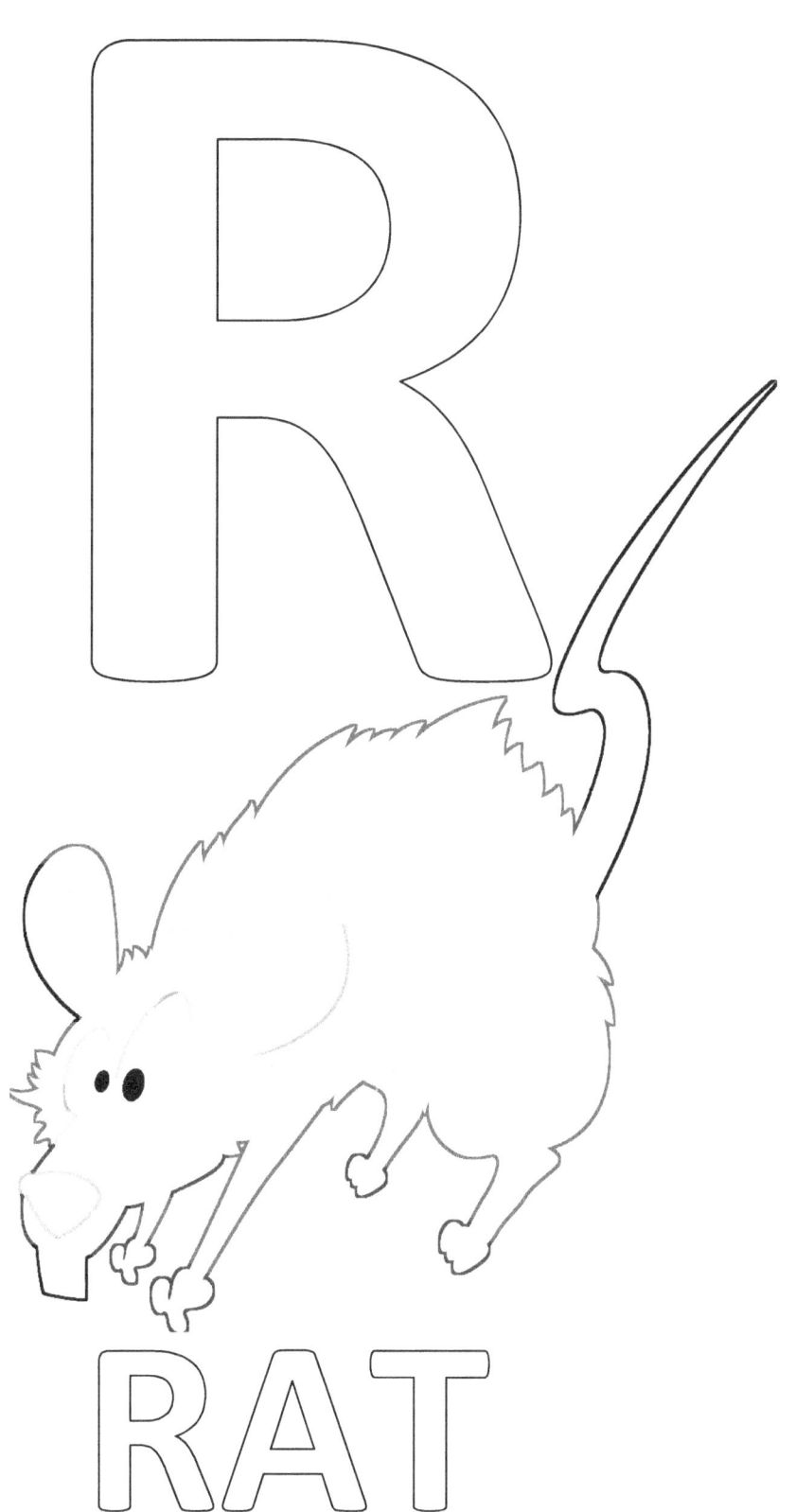

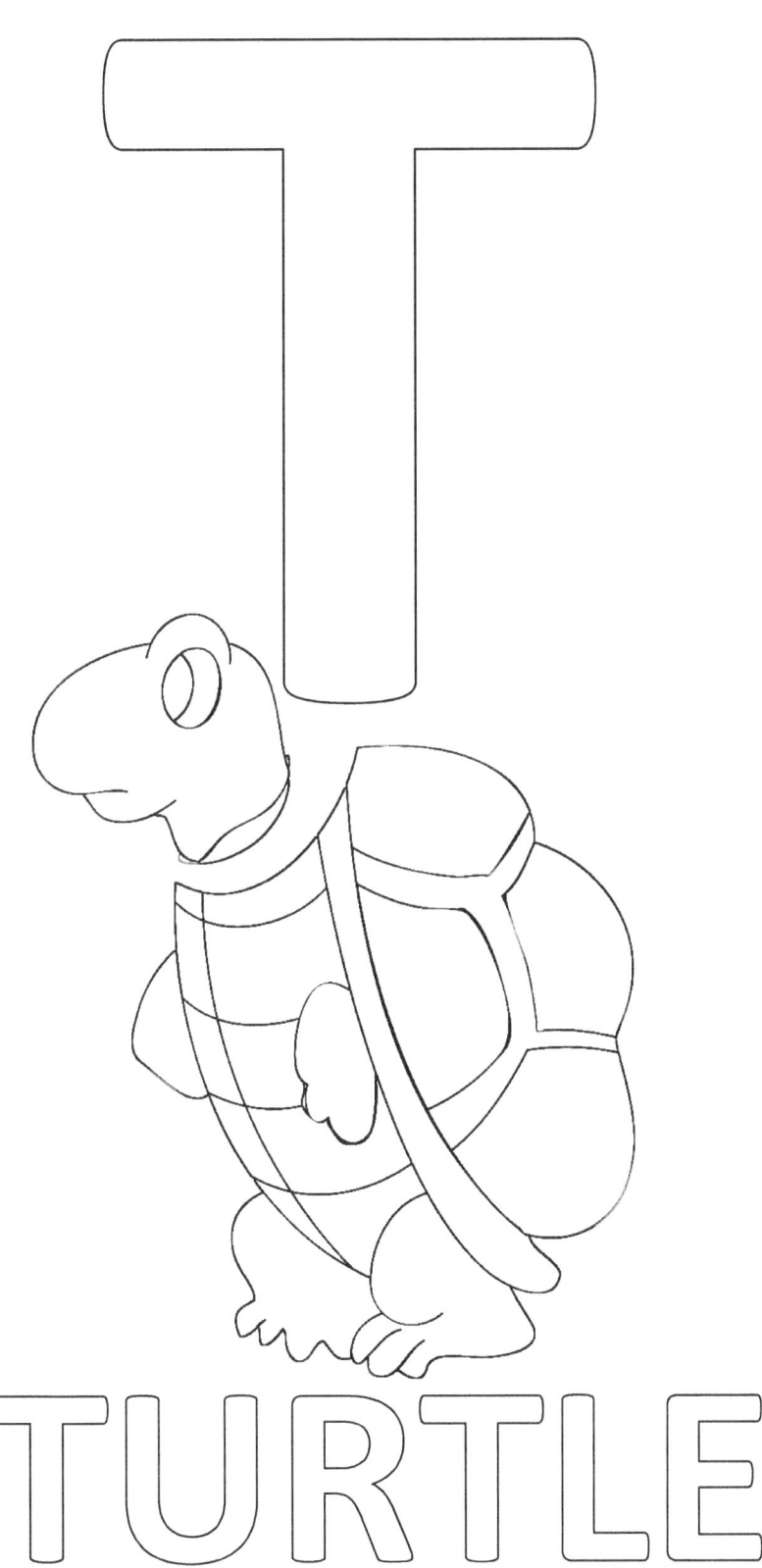

TURTLE

U

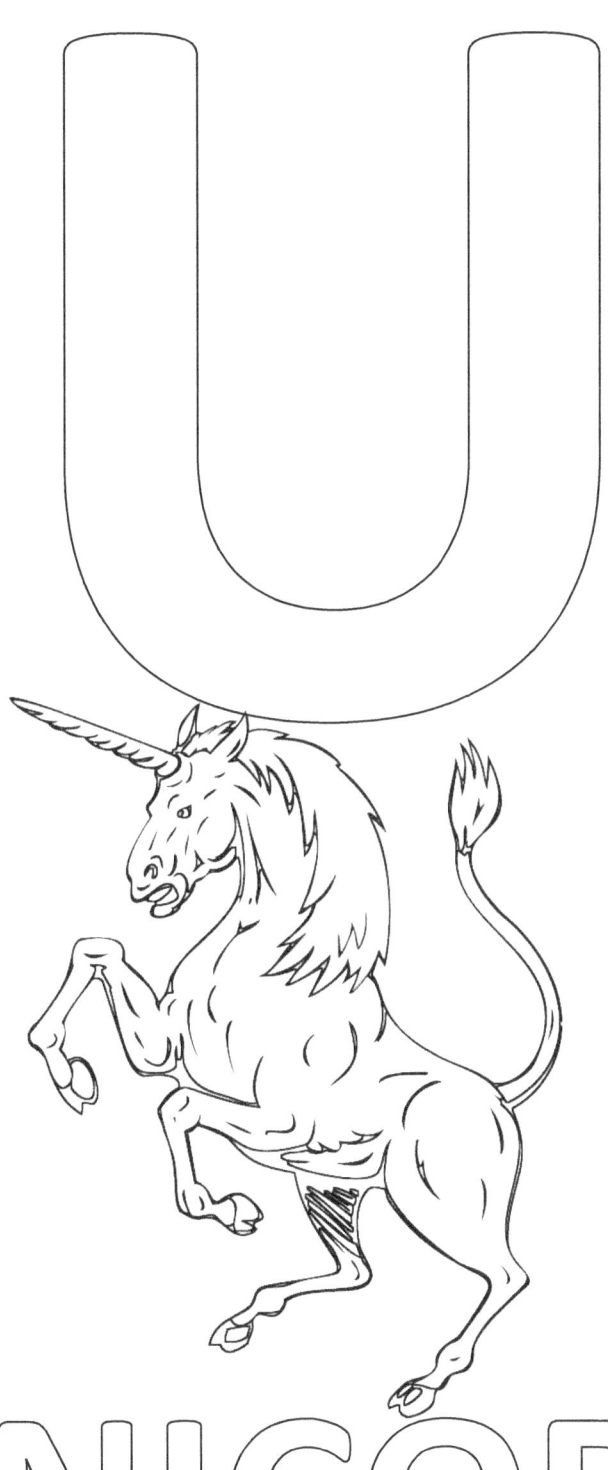

UNICORN

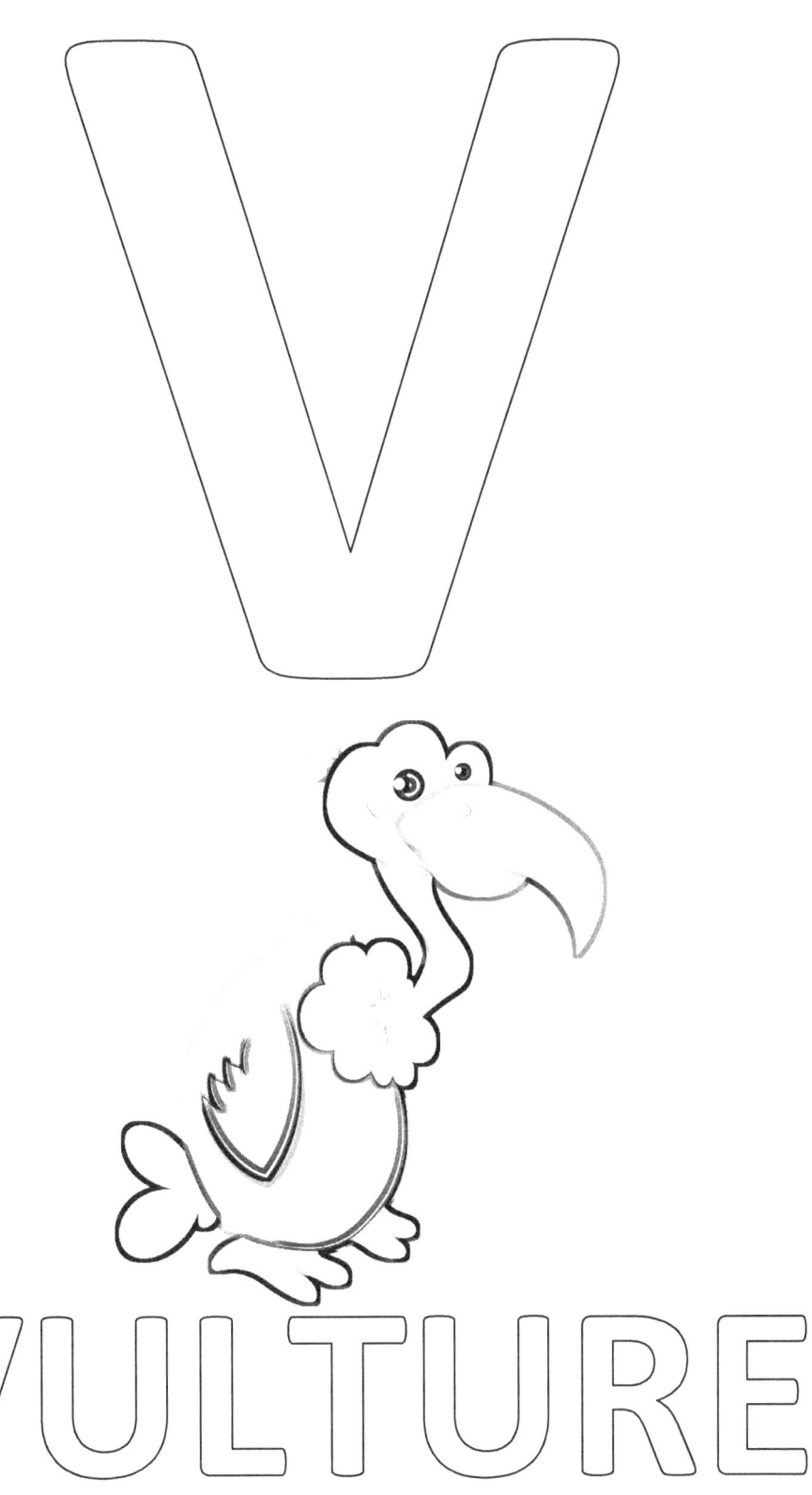

VULTURE

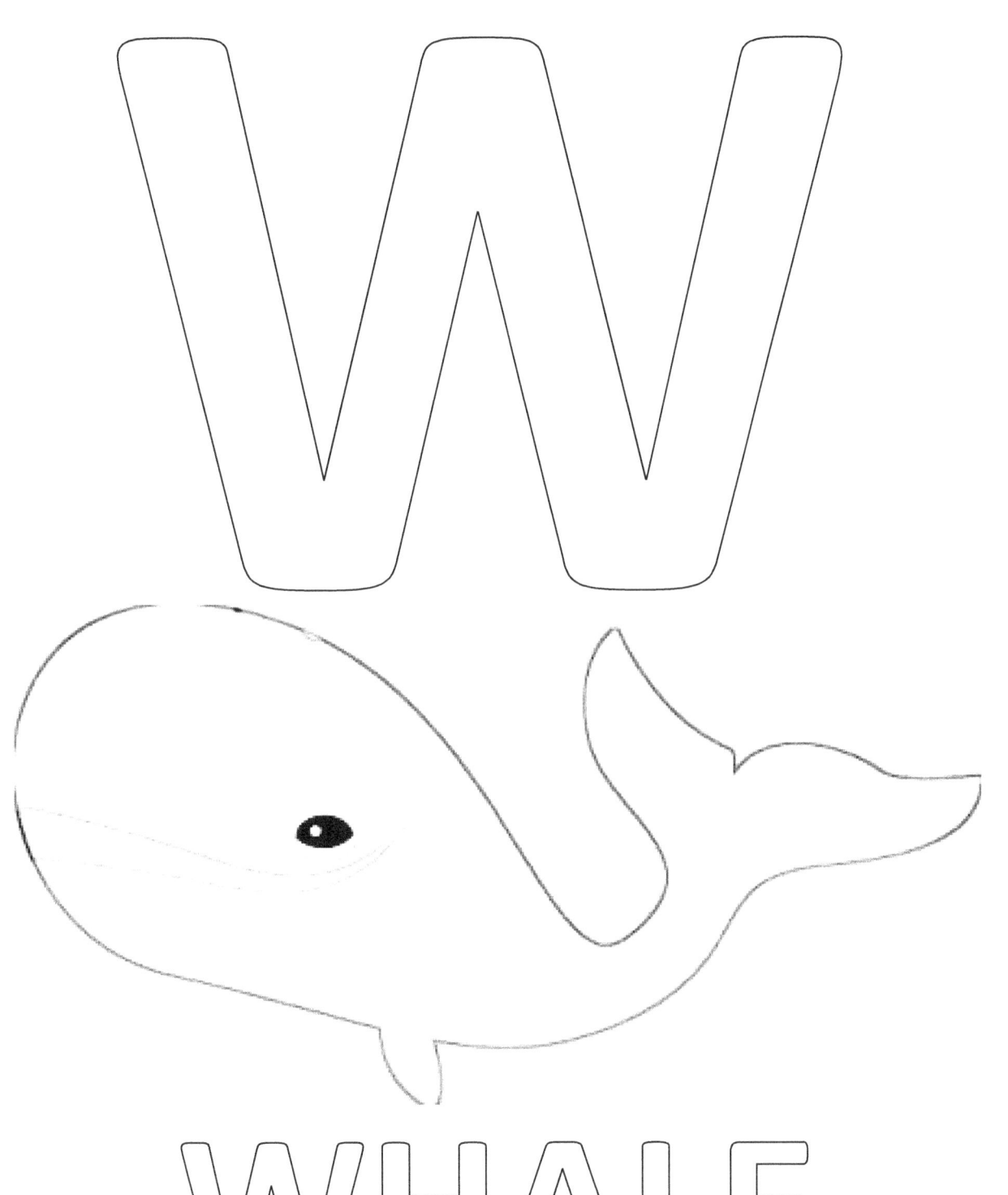

WHALE

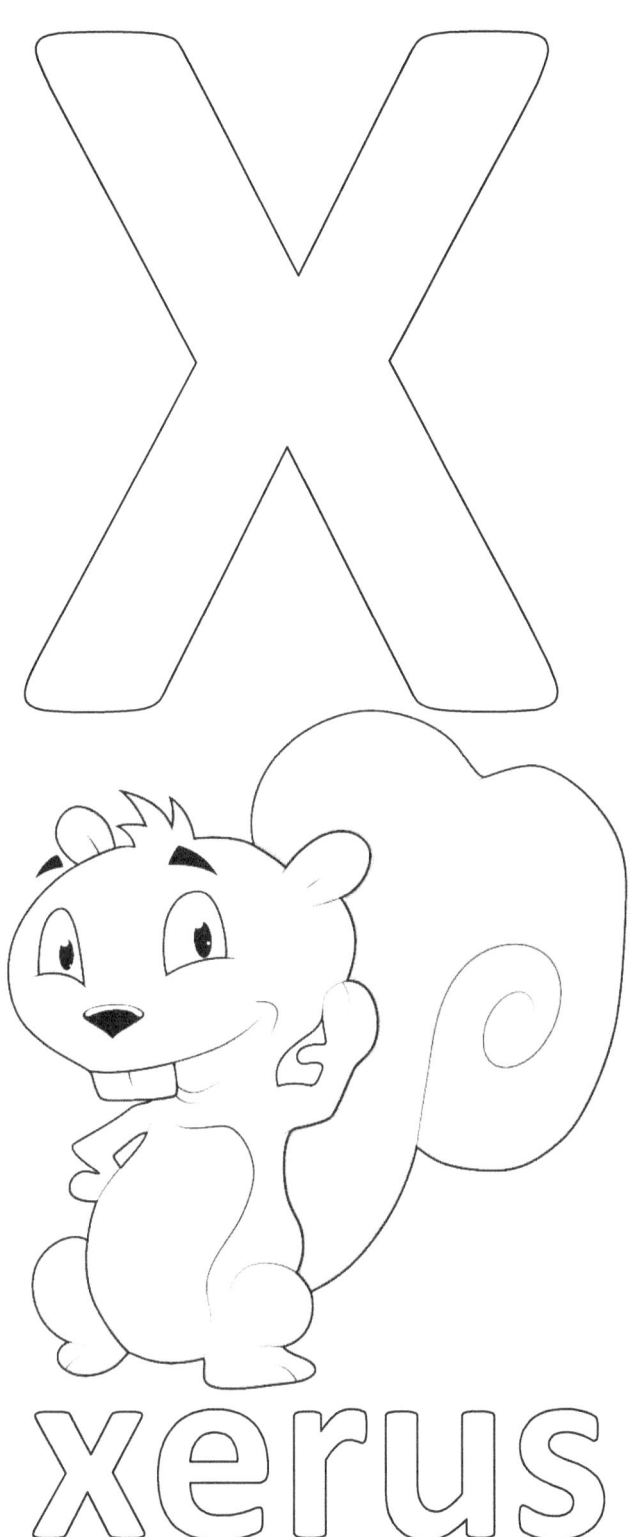

xerus

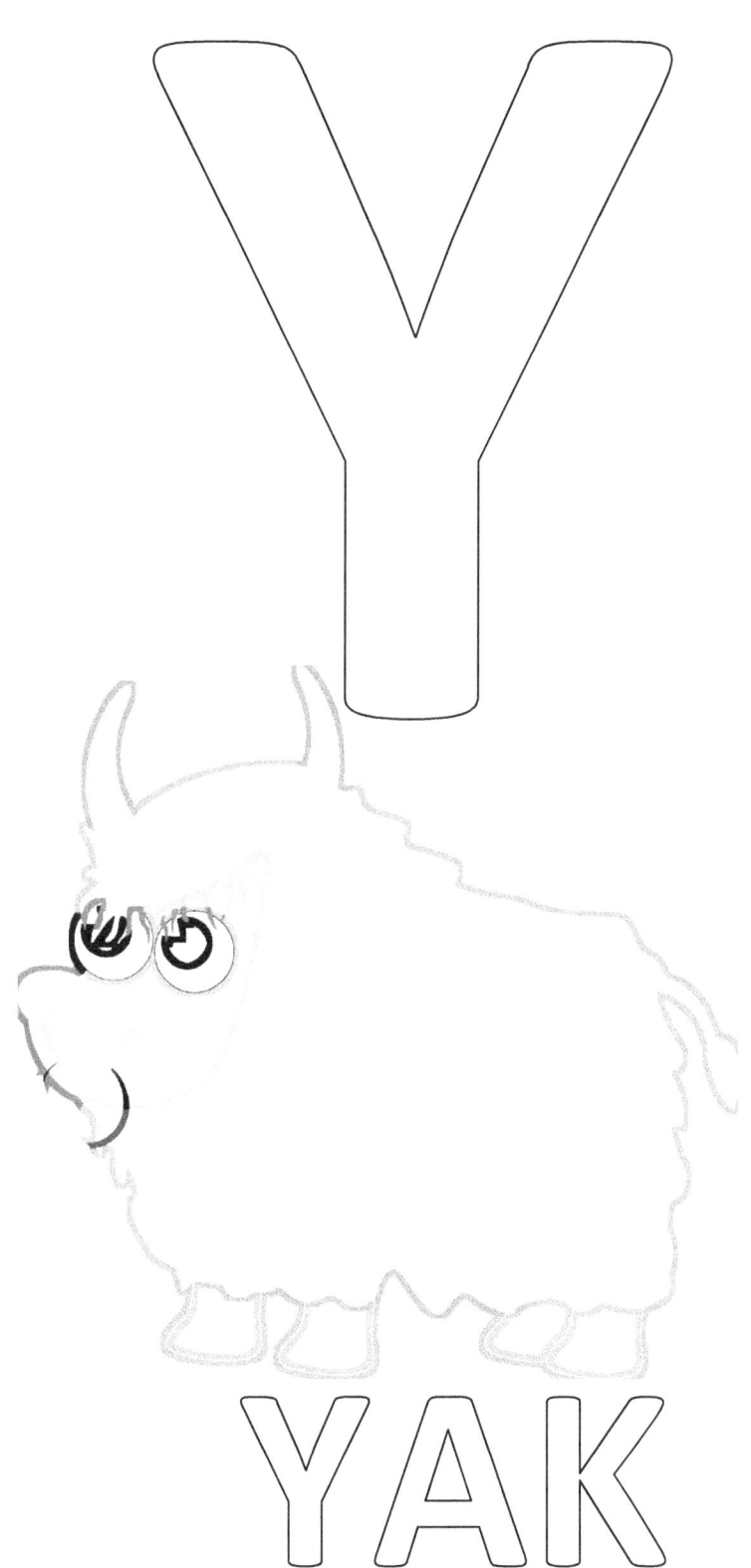

YAK

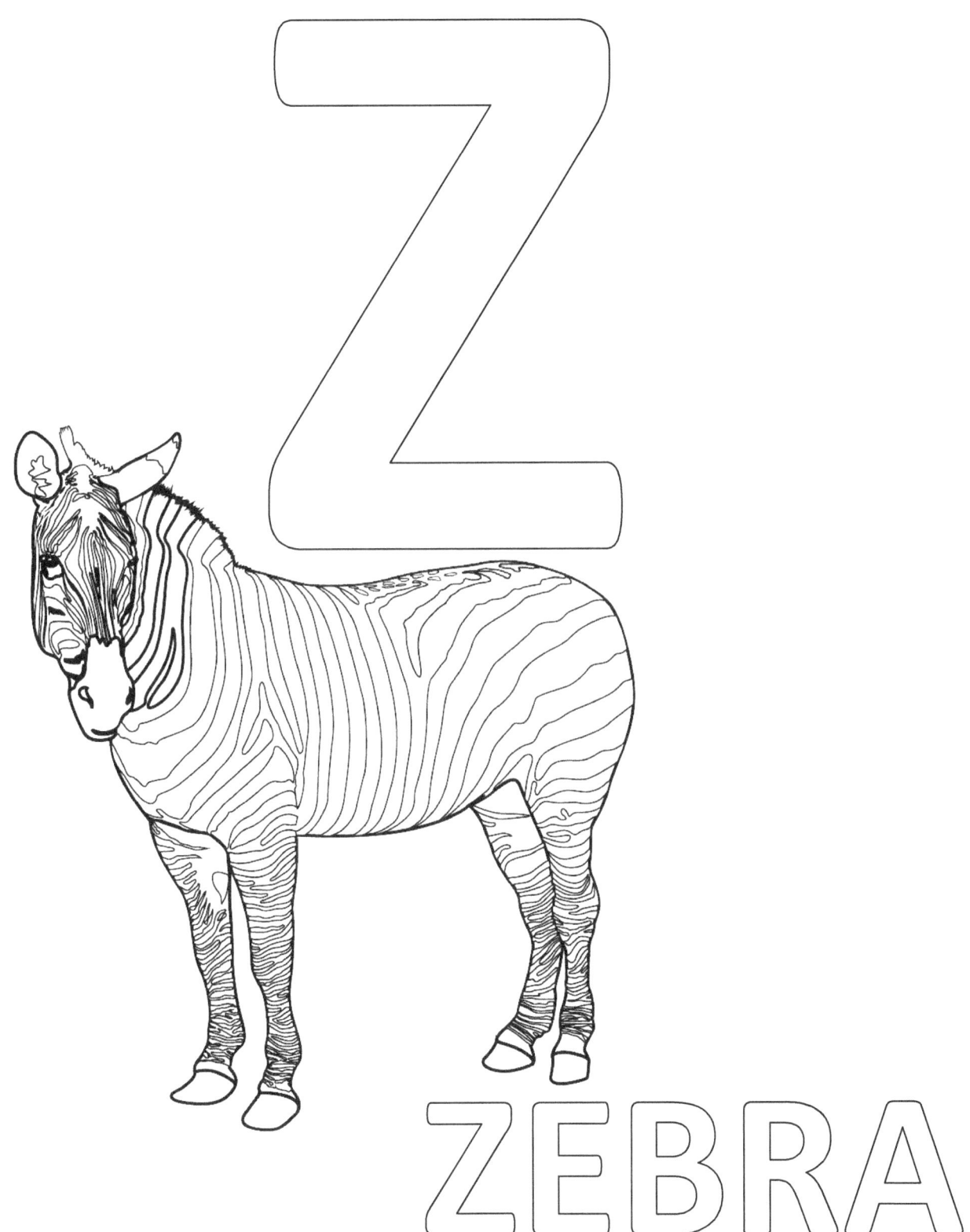

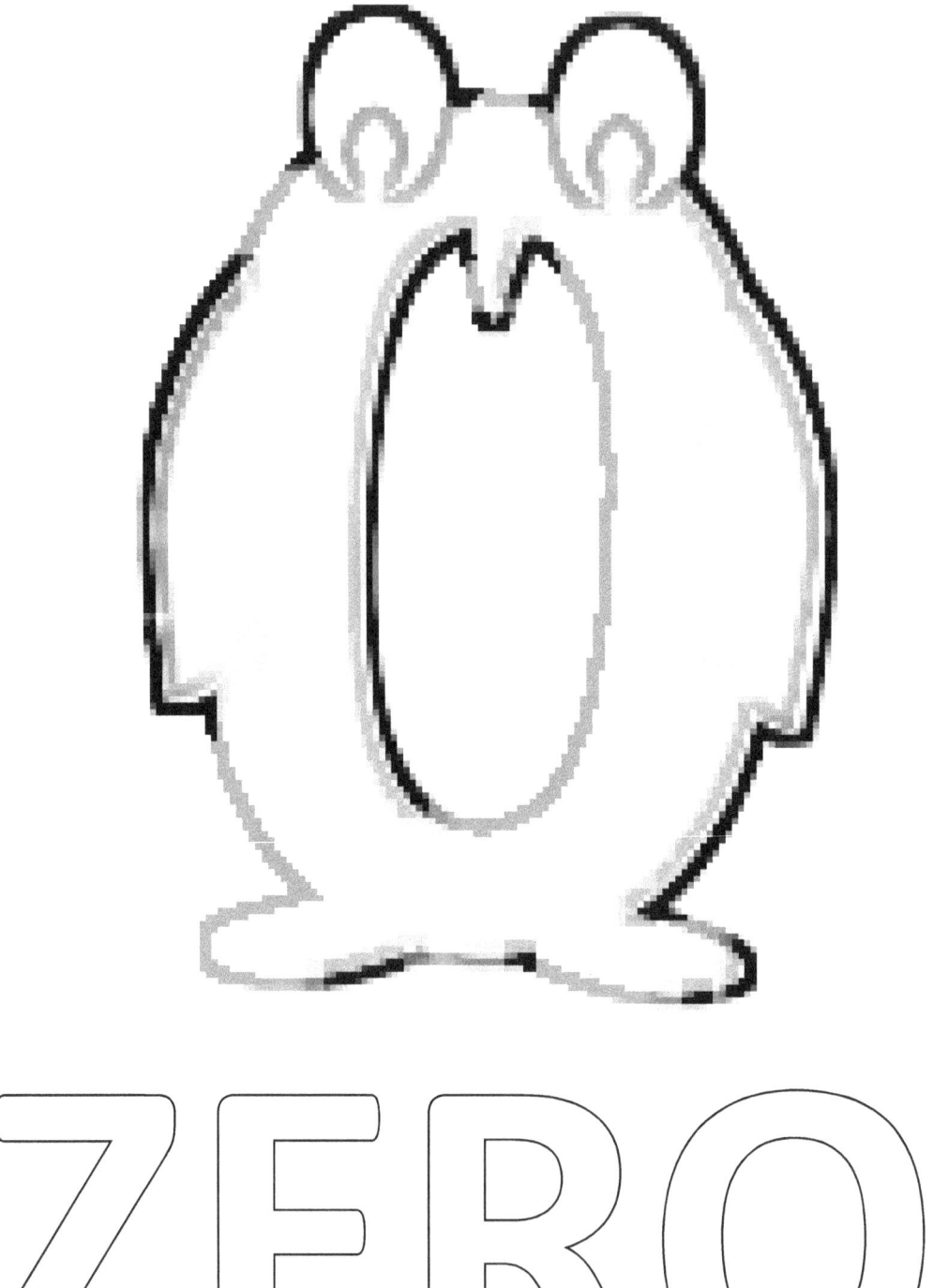

ZERO

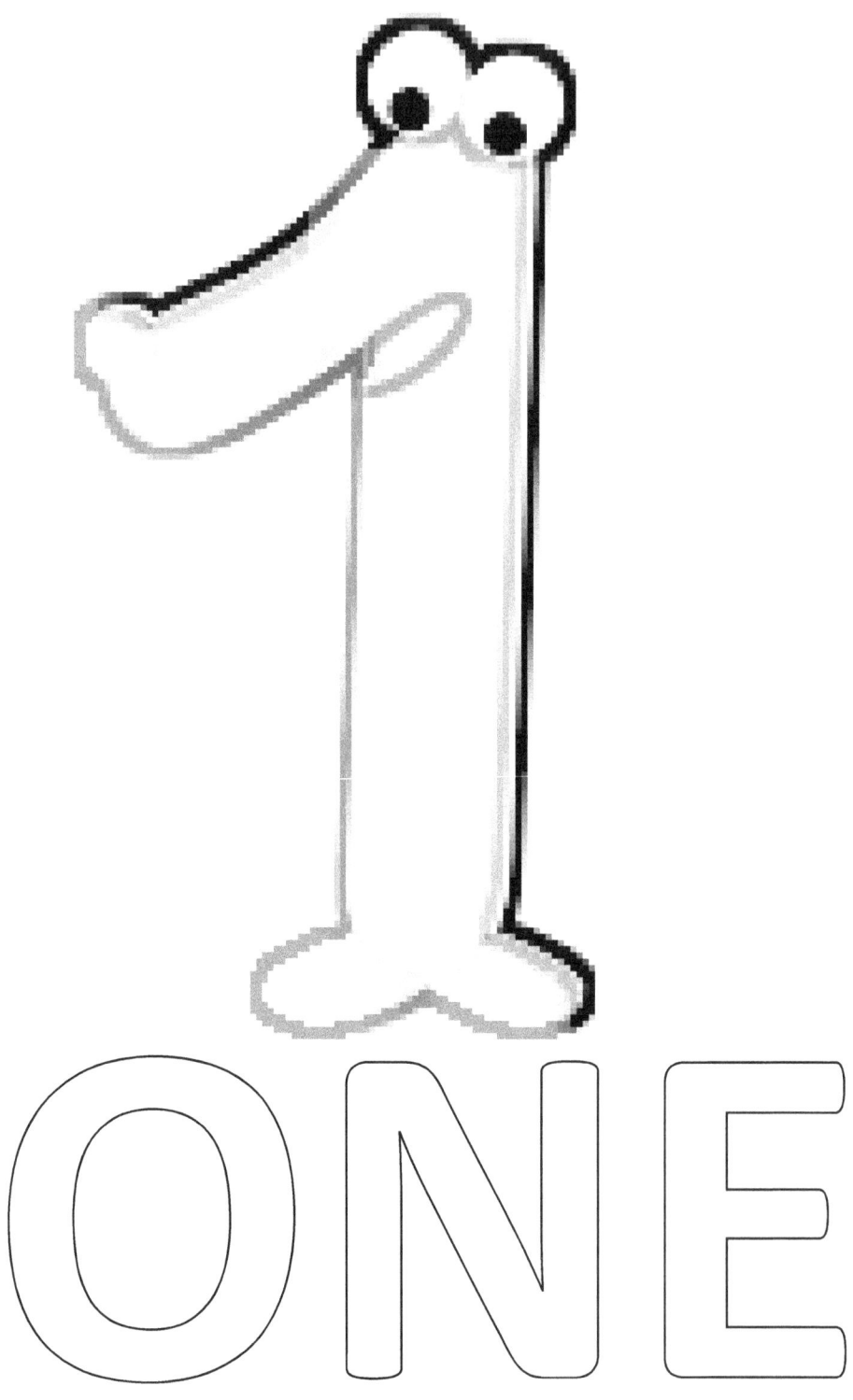

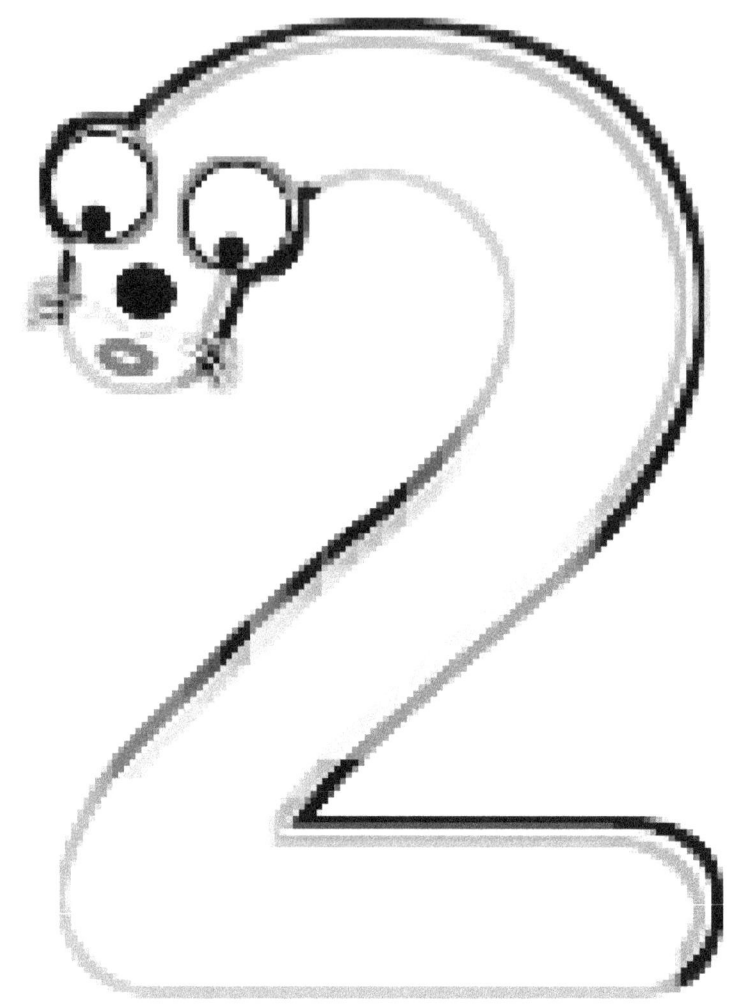

TWO

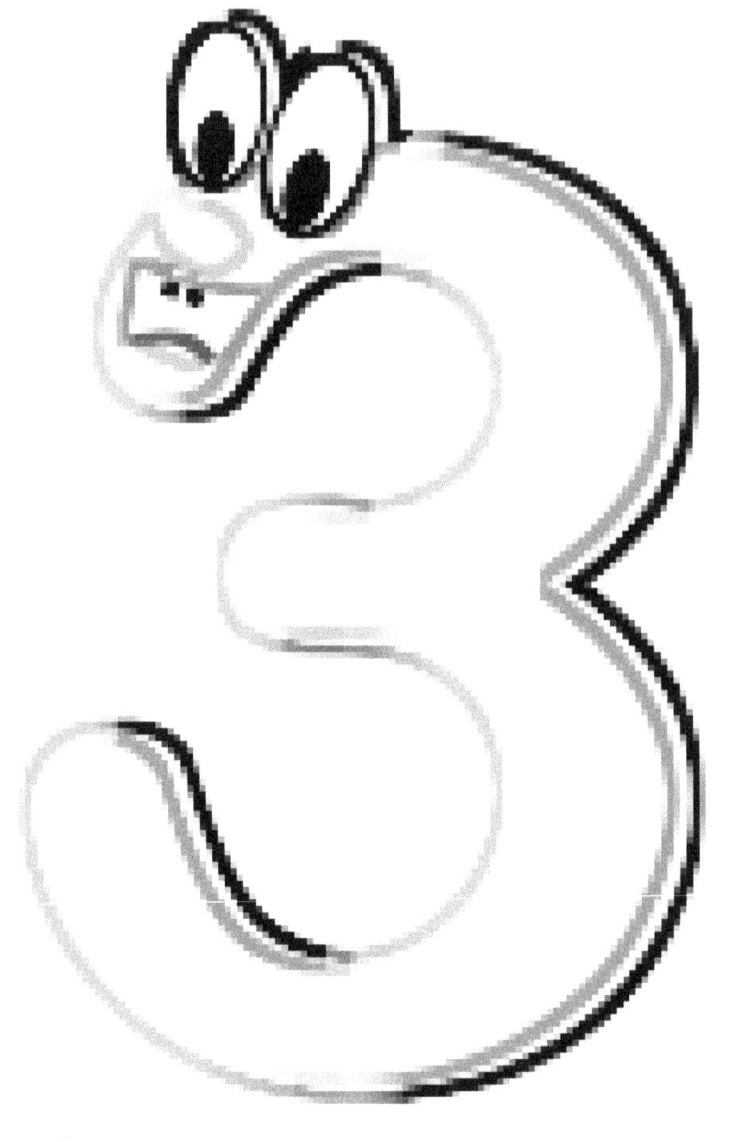

THREE

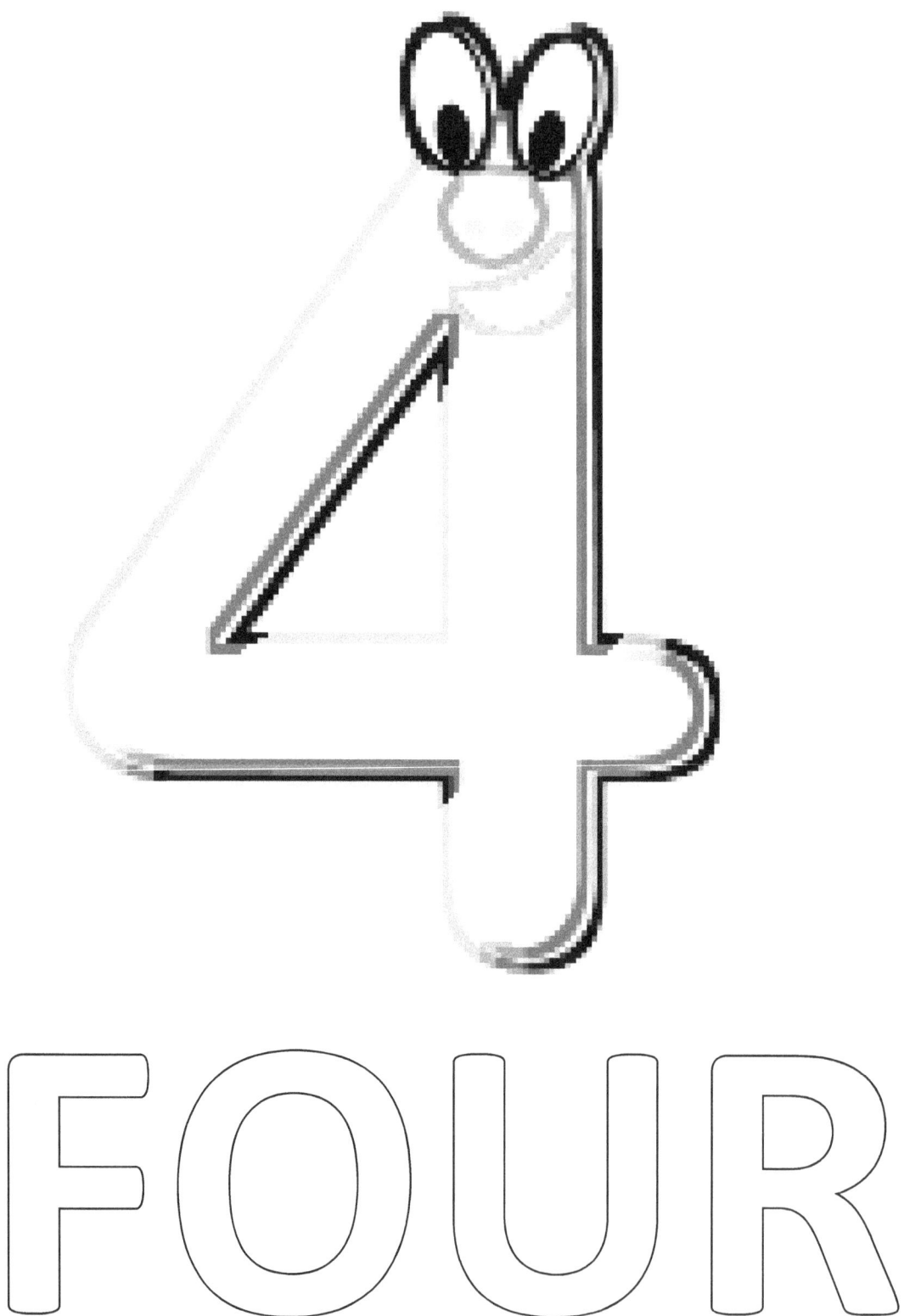

FOUR

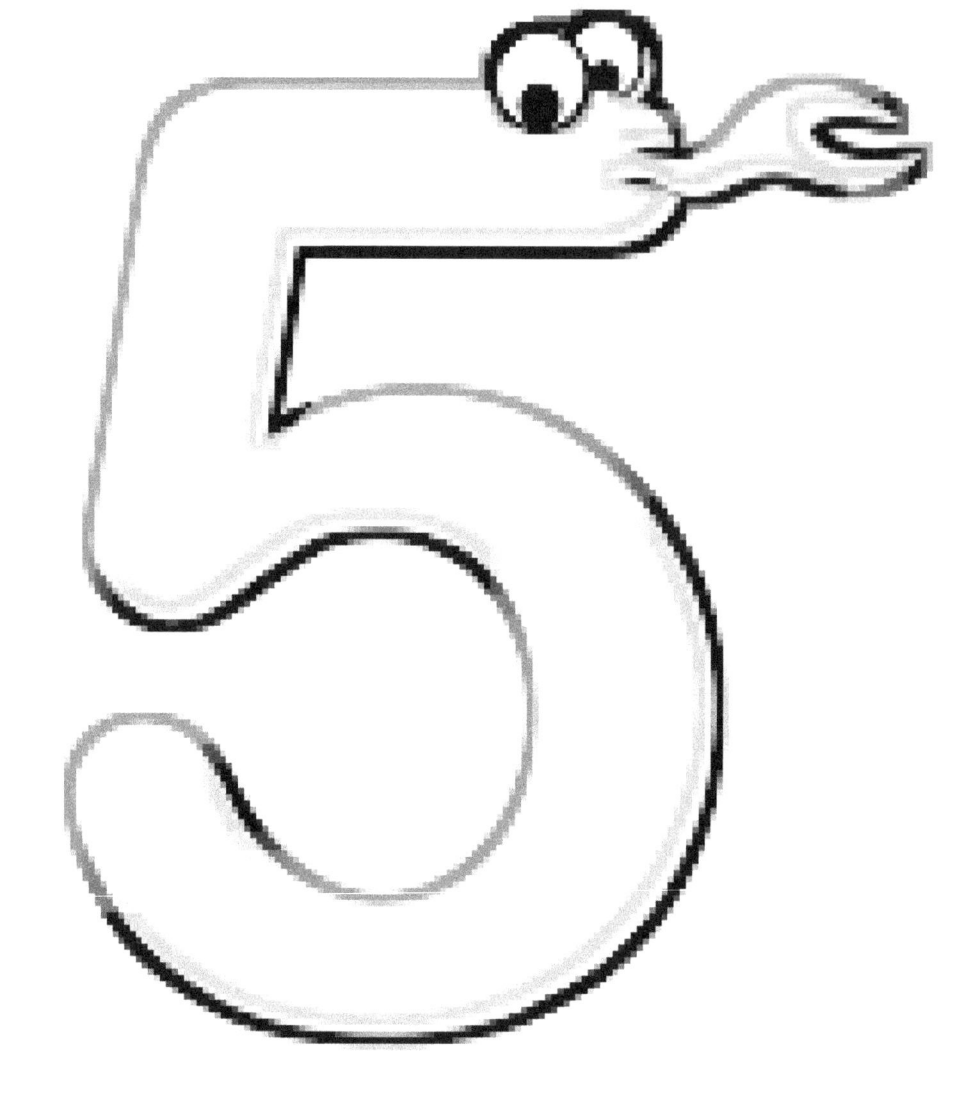

FIVE

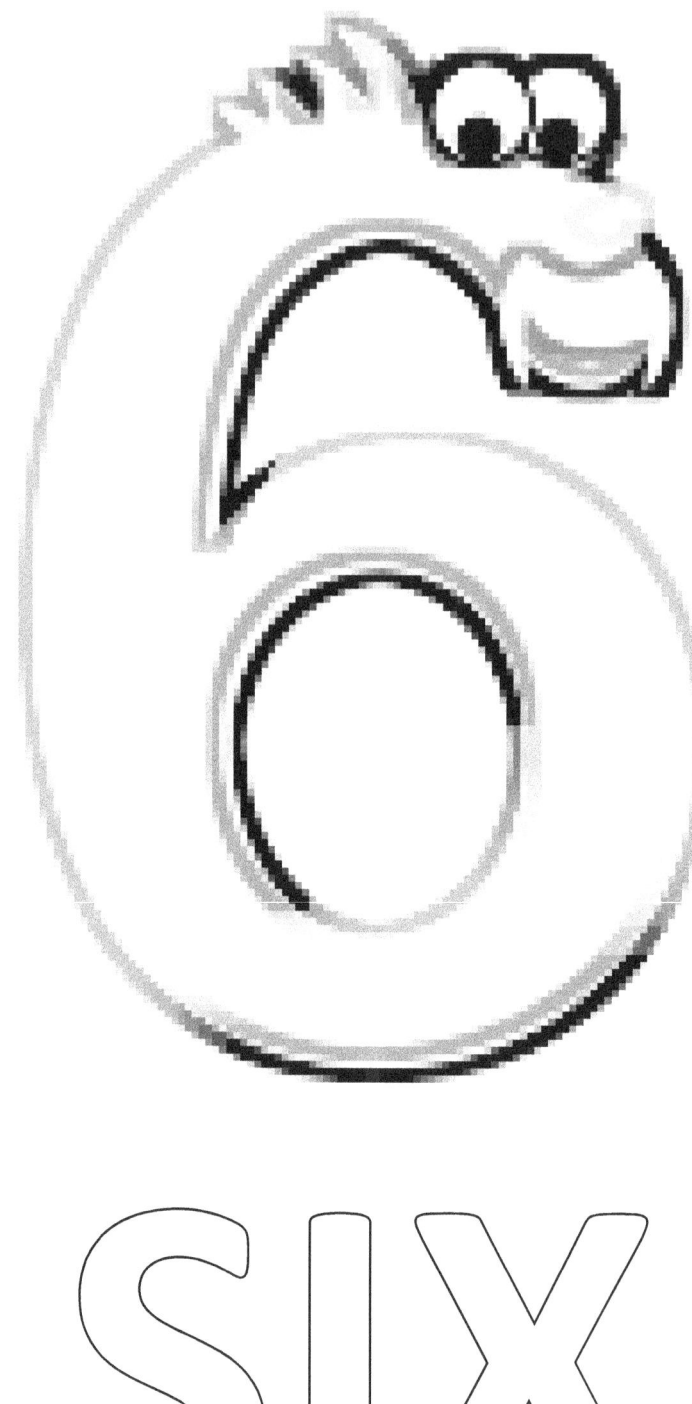

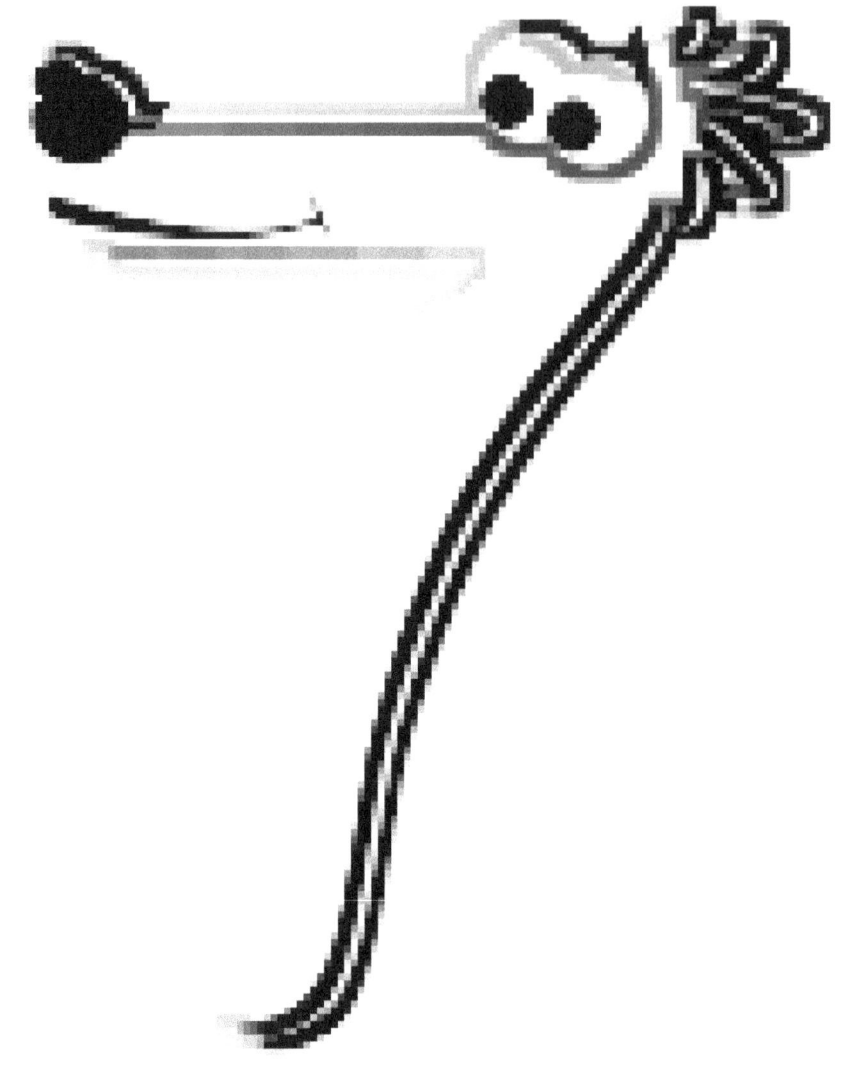

SEVEN

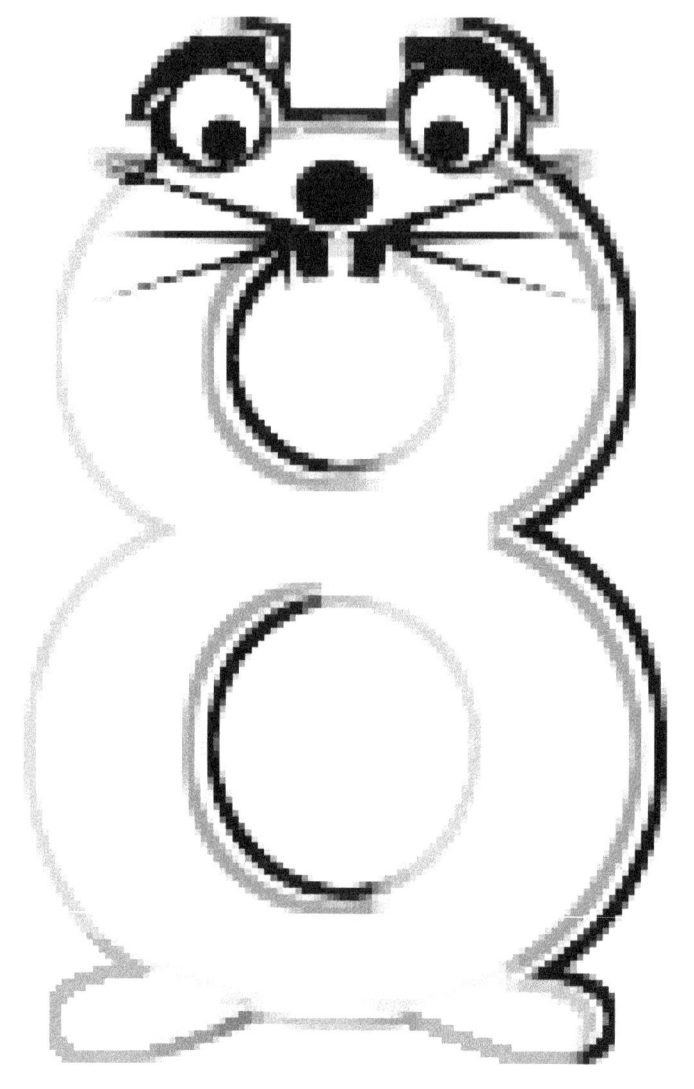

EIGHT

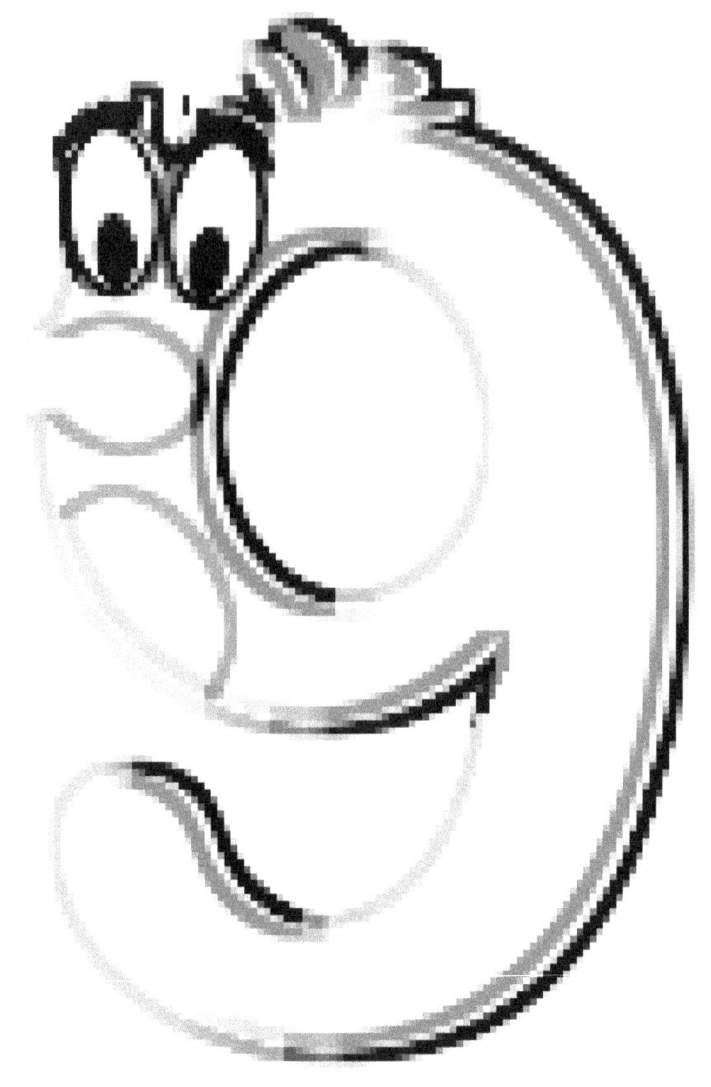

NINE

Thank you

Hope you've enjoyed your reading experience.
We here at T.Michelle will always strive to deliver to you the highest quality guides.
So I'd like to thank you for supporting us and reading until the very end.
Before you go, would you mind leaving us a review on Amazon?
It will mean a lot to us and support us creating high quality guides for you in the future.
Thanks once again and here's where you can leave a review.
Get Free Ebook Coloring Page below
Best Book By T. Michelle
(fb.com/groups/1523056898003358)

Warmly yours,
T.Michelle Team